GOOGLE CLOUD CERTIFIED

Google Professional Cloud Architect and Google Professional Data Engineer study guide

2 books in 1

By

Jason Hoffman

Edition 2020

Table of contents

GOOGLE PROFESSIONAL DATA ENGINEERING

Disclaimer

The content of this book has been checked and compiled with great care. For the completeness, correctness and topicality of the contents however no guarantee or guarantee can be taken over. The content of this book represents the personal experience and opinion of the author and is for entertainment purposes only. The content should not be confused with medical help.

There will be no legal responsibility or liability for damages resulting from counterproductive exercise or errors by the reader. No guarantee can be given for success. The author therefore assumes no responsibility for the non-achievement of the goals described in the book.

CHAPTER ONE - GOOGLE PROFESSIONAL DATA ENGINEERING OVERVIEW

What Is Data Engineering?

Data engineering.

Data Engineering (IE), otherwise called Data Technology Engineering (ITE), data building procedure (IEM), or data designing, is a product designing way to deal with planning and creating data systems.

Review

Data Technology Engineering (ITE) includes a building approach for arranging, dissecting, planning, and actualizing applications. Steven M Davis has characterized ITE as: "An incorporated and developmental arrangement of undertakings and methods that improve business correspondence all through an endeavor empowering it to create individuals, techniques, and systems to accomplish its vision."

ITE has numerous reasons, including association arranging, business re-designing, application improvement, information systems arranging, and systems re-designing. ITE can be utilized to break down, plan, and execute information structures in an undertaking. ITE's objective is to consider a business to improve how it deals with its assets, for example, capital, individuals, and information systems to accomplish its business objectives. The significance of ITE and its ideas have expanded quickly with the development of current innovation. ITE accept that coherent information portrayals are steady; which is the inverse to the cycles that utilization the information, which continually change; this takes into consideration the legitimate information model, which mirrors an association's thoughts, to be the reason for the development of systems

History

Data technology engineering used to be known more commonly as data engineering; this changed in the early 21st century, and data engineering took on a new meaning.

Data technology designing has a somewhat checkered history that follows two exceptionally particular strings. It began in Australia somewhere in 1976 and 1980 and appeared first in the literature in a series of Six in-depth articles by the same name published by the US Computer world in May - June 1981. Data technology engineering first gave data examination and data set plan methods that could be utilized by database overseers (DBAs) and systems investigators to create data set plans and systems dependent on a comprehension of the operational preparing needs of associations 1980s.

Clive Finkelstein is recognized as the "Father" of data technology engineering, having built up its ideas from 1976 to 1980, dependent on his unique work to connect from a key business wanting to data systems. He composed the primary distribution on data technology designing: a progression of six inside and out articles of a similar name distributed by the US Computer world in May - June 1981. He likewise co-composed with James Martin, the persuasive Savant Institute Report named: "Data Engineering," distributed in Nov 1981. The Finkelstein string advanced from 1976 as the business-driven variation of ITE. The Martin string advanced into the data preparing is driven (DP) variation of ITE. From 1983 till 1986, ITE developed further into a more grounded business-driven ITE interpretation, which was expected to address a quickly changing business condition. The then specialized chief, Charles M. Richter, from 1983 to 1987, guided by Clive Finkelstein, assumed an essential function by redoing the ITE system just as assisting with planning the ITE programming item (client data) which computerized the ITE technique, opening the best approach to cutting edge Data Architecture.

The Martin string was data base plan-driven from the beginning, and 1983 was centered around the chance of robotizing the improvement cycle through the arrangement of methods for a business depiction that could be utilized to populate a data word reference or reference book that could, thus, be used as source material for code age. The Martin procedure gave an establishment to the CASE (PC helped programming building) device industry. Martin himself had critical stakes in any event four CASE tools merchants - InTech (Excelerator), Higher-Order Software, KnowledgeWare, initially Database Design Inc, Data Engineering Workbench and James Martin Associates, initially DMW and now Headstrong (the first architects of the Texas Instruments' CA Gen and the main engineers of the system).

Toward the finish of the 1980s and mid-1990s, the Martin string consolidated rapid application development (RAD) and business measure reengineering (BPR) and not long after additionally entered the article situated field. Over this equivalent period, the Finkelstein string advanced further into Enterprise Architecture (EA). His business-driven ITE techniques developed into Enterprise Engineering for the fast conveyance of EA, which is portrayed in his books: "Endeavor Architecture for Integration: Rapid Delivery Methods and Technologies." First release by Clive Finkelstein (2006) in hardcover. The subsequent release (2011) is in PDF and as an iBook on the Apple iPad and digital book on the Amazon Kindle.

As organizations advanced along in the public eye, so did the requirement for data designing practices to be actualized in a far-reaching way to build profitability, proficiency, and benefits among organizations. Everything a business jar quite often are helped by technology in some way. It is the place the philosophy of data designing gets significant. Organizations will consistently have issues to settle, and the development of technology helped by the data building approach has brought perhaps the best thing to occur in the business world. Issues that physically must be finished by hand should now be possible by PC, for example, finance and advantages for an organization. Utilizing data building to tackle issues can spare time, cash, and lessen the chance of human blunder.

The phase of Data Engineering

- Strategic Business Planning: Business targets that heads set for what's to come are portrayed in key marketable strategies, with their more important definition in strategic marketable plans and usage in operational field-tested strategies. Most organizations today perceive the crucial need to grow a marketable process that follows this procedure. It is frequently hard to execute these plans due to the associations' strategic and operational degrees' absence of straightforwardness. This sort of arrangement expects the input to consider early revision of issues because of miscommunication and distortion of their strategy.

- Data Modeling: The ideal reason for data models is founded on bearings made by the control for the business's eventual fate. Marketable strategies characterize these headings. Data models can give a reasonable understanding of future business needs when field-tested strategies become inaccessible or outdated. Data models can be created from any announcement of strategy, objective, target, or system for a business and its needs. After some time, data that has been reliably refreshed can help a business perceive how things have changed and how the business requirements are diverse going ahead.

- Process Modeling: Process demonstrating is like data displaying as in it is investigating the cycles a business has required sketched out by its marketable strategy, utilizing a data designing methodology, cycles can be connected to data and necessities, to improve the feeling of why the process exists and how it must be done, this considers a business to get a review of what it is as of now doing, and why it is doing the things it is doing, the significance of everything, and how these things are being finished.

- Systems Design and Implementation: The fourth and last period of data building is systems plan and usage. After setting a field-tested strategy, data models are utilized to make measure models, which are then used to plan systems, so they are prepared for execution. This stage is the completing stage. The systems plan and execution stage takes what has been made by the past three periods of data designing and wraps everything into one last item. Hence, it is accessible to be actualized, and this is the place organizations can see the summit of their data building stages and endeavors.

Data technology building points

ITE variations

There are two variations of data technology building. These are known as the DP-driven variation and the business-driven variation.

- DP-driven: The DP-driven variation of data technology building was intended to empower data systems divisions to create data systems that fulfilled the data needs of the 1980s. These necessities were generally a DP-driven improvement condition. The vast majority of the CASE tools accessible today uphold this DP-driven variation of ITE.

- Business-driven: ITE was reached out into key business anticipating the business-driven variation of data technology designing. This variation was intended for a quick change in the customer/worker, an item arranged condition of the business-driven 1990s.

Business-driven ITE is recorded in the later books by Clive Finkelstein.

DP-driven Variant of ITE

- Data Strategy Planning: The basic goal of Data Strategy Planning (ISP) is to build up an arrangement for executing business systems to help business needs. The current systems scene is contrasted with the aspirations communicated in the current field-tested strategy, and a few developments anticipate for new or improved systems are distinguished.

- Outline Business Area Analysis: For every improvement venture, business examiners characterize the business cycles and data possibly required in the new framework. These are demonstrated utilizing measure disintegration graphs, measure reliance charts, and substance relationship models.

- Detailed Business Area Analysis: The reason for a DBAA stage is to give point by point models a strong basis for framework plans. Cycles have deteriorated to rudimentary business measures, and the business rationale of the processes is communicated in data activities against the completely standardized data model. This way, the cycle and data models are tried against each other before development.

- Business System Design: The reason for a Business System Design venture is to indicate all parts of a framework that apply to its clients, anticipating the specialized plan, development, and establishment of at least one firmly related databases and systems. The rudimentary cycles are planned into methods that can be executed by clients. Unambiguous and predictable determinations with the volume of detail important to settle on arranging and specialized plan choices are readied.

- Technical Design: A Technical Design venture readies an execution territory for development and establishment. The key assignments are organized to create a framework and database that meets the client's acknowledgment models and is sound.

- Construction: The goal of the Construction stage is to deliver a framework, as characterized in the specialized particular, on schedule, and inside spending plan. The framework should be of adequate quality and contain all important working and client techniques. The assignment is finished when the acknowledgment models for the business framework are met.

- Transition: Transition is characterized as the period during which recently created methods steadily supplant or are interfaced with existing strategies. The execution of a Transition venture requests exhaustive comprehension of both the framework to be introduced and the systems to be replaced. Business driven ITE Variant for fast Delivery

- Strategy Analysis: This is a fast conveyance strategy for ranking directors and specialty unit administrators to refine existing vital techniques or improve new critical strategies if none exists yet.

- Strategic Modeling: This uses an encouraging demonstrating meeting with senior business directors who audit the vital field-tested strategies to build up an essential model, and this is a venture data model where many-to-numerous affiliations have been deteriorated to recognize the need business exercises and cycles distinguished by the control, this uses substance reliance analysis to consequently determine venture plans and task maps from the vital model. It brings about reusable processes for fast conveyance into creation as coordinated databases and reusable systems.

- Tactical and Operational Modeling: This uses a similar methodology concerning key displaying, yet centers around strategic specialty units - venturing into strategic quality detail and later operational characteristic detail for physical database age and establishment.

- Activity Modeling: Activity models, in light of IDEF0 and movement-based costing, are utilized to report need business exercises for fast conveyance.

- Process Modeling: Business Process Modeling Notation (BPMN) is utilized, upheld by demonstrating instruments, to characterize measure model graphs in BPMN of need exercises for fast conveyance into creation.

- Code Generation: BPMN measure model outlines are utilized to produce XML-based code in Business Process Execution Language (BPEL) for execution.

ITE methods

A few methods that are utilized during an ITE venture are:

- Entity examination: recognizes all the things that the undertaking might need to hold data about. The analysis arranges everything into various substance types, uncovering how they identify with one another, depicted in the element model.
- Function analysis and cycle reliance: takes a capacity (a significant business movement) of the venture and separates it into rudimentary business measures. From this, two charts are readied: the cycle deterioration graph, which shows the breakdown of business work, and the cycle reliance outline, which shows the interdependencies of business measures.
- Process rationale analysis: portrays the arrangements of activities did by a business cycle and shows which each activity utilizes data.
- Entity type lifecycle analysis: portrays the noteworthy business changes to elements and affirm that cycles have been displayed to impact these progressions
- Matrix cross-checking: makes cross-references between data articles and cycles to confirm that they are vital and complete.
- Normalization: gives a proper method for affirming the rightness of the element model.
- Cluster examination: characterizes the extent of plan zones for proposed business systems.
- Datastream and data examination: make a correlation conceivable between the business territory models and the

systems supporting this zone. These current systems are investigated utilizing data stream and data examination methods.

The collaboration of devices and data designing

A significant perspective in the improvement of data building, utilizing PCs to help with the planning cycle, empowered the capacity to handle more significant and more intricate issues. This development went along because of the absence of mental ability controlled by people to tackle these perplexing issues that necessary an excessive amount of data to be held by the human mind. A few instances of this are definitions, designs, character portrayals, report necessities, and identifiers. For the most part, these are instances of data that are preferred put away on PCs over in the human cerebrum. Alongside the data, visual angles to speak to these snippets of data were also required, further expanding the requirement for a technology-based answer for this issue.

During the 1980s, PCs started to be considerably more generally utilized in the business universes. This wonder prompted the requirement for data more quickly and proficiently. This development of data designing took into consideration choices to be made faster, data to be found quicker, reports to be made faster, and an exchange reaction faster. Even though speed was an essential factor in how these organizations got things done, the data actually must be exact, which made a 'race' between organizations, to see which had the best data in the quickest time utilizing a minimal measure of assets.

This development prompted the possibility of robotization. Mechanization took into account these cycles to be immediately managed without a lot of any human data. This sped up brought down incorrectness and expanded proficiency. The data building approach has been developing quickly in the previous years as it has been demonstrated to be extraordinary compared to other development techniques.

Data building as a field of study and profession

With the enormous improvement of technology as of late, data designing has gotten progressively famous. The ideas driving data building are educated as right on time as primary school and as late as bosses and Ph.D. programs inside the field of data designing. This fame increment has prompted a broad blast in the number of individuals who can work in areas that are intensely data building based. Data building has become its very own professional way and a significant rewarding one, also. Data engineers procure a regular pay of $106,000, as indicated by Glassdoor. Many top schools and colleges offer data building programs too.

Programming tools

There are a few tools supporting data technology designing

- CA Gen from Texas Instruments Software; this was offered to Sterling Software and afterward to Computer Associates. It exists in an advanced structure inside the Advantage suite. In 2006, alluded to as ALL: Fusion Gen, fit for creating J2EE and JAVA web applications notwithstanding inheritance customer/worker and centralized computer stages.

- Metastorm's ProVision item offers help for some sorts of displaying strategies utilizing a vault based instrument.

- Microsoft Visio gives graphing backing to some diagrammatic procedures, such as ER displaying Crow's foot documentation, data stream charting, measure demonstrating, and swimlane outlines.

Different devices incorporate Bachman's Data Analyst, Excelerator, and then some. See PC supported programming designing.

The Google Cloud Platform

Google Cloud Platform (GCP), made by Google, is a set-up of distributed computing services that sudden spikes in demand for a similar infrastructure that Google utilizes inside for its end-client items, for example, Google Search, Gmail, and YouTube. Close by many control devices gives a progression of private cloud services, including processing, data storage, data analysis, and AI. Enrollment requires a charge card or ledger subtleties.

Google Cloud Platform

Owner	Google
Industry	Web service, cloud computing
URL	cloud.google.com
Launched	April 7, 2008; 12 years ago
Current status	Active
Written in	• Java • C++ • Python • Go • Ruby

Google Cloud Platform gives infrastructure as assistance, stage as a help, and serverless computing conditions.

In April 2008, Google reported App Engine, a stage for creating and facilitating web applications in Google-oversaw server farms, the principal distributed computing administration. The administration turned out to be commonly accessible in November 2011. Since the declaration of the App Engine, Google added various cloud services to the stage.

Google Cloud Platform is a Google Cloud piece, which incorporates the Google Cloud Platform public cloud framework, just as G Suite, undertaking adaptations of Android and Chrome OS, and application programming interfaces (APIs) for AI and endeavor planning services.

Items

Google records more than 90 items under the Google Cloud brand. A portion of the key services is recorded beneath.

Register

- Application Engine - Platform as a Service to send Java, PHP, Node.js, Python, C#, .Net, Go applications, and Ruby.
- Compute Engine - Infrastructure as a Service to run Linux virtual machines and Microsoft Windows.
- Kubernetes Engine (GKE) or GKE on-prem offered as an element of Anthos stage
- Containers as a Service subject to Kubernetes.
- Cloud Functions - Functions as a Service to run event-driven code written in Node.js, Python, or Go.
- Cloud Run - Compute execution condition dependent on Knative. They were offered as Cloud Run (ultimately oversaw) or as Cloud Run for Anthos.

Capacity and Databases

- Cloud Storage - Object storage with incorporated edge reserving to store unstructured data.
- Cloud SQL - Database as a Service dependent on MySQL and PostgreSQL.
- Cloud Bigtable - Managed NoSQL database assistance.
- Cloud Spanner - Horizontally adaptable, unequivocally predictable, social database assistance.
- Cloud Datastore - NoSQL database for web and portable applications.
- Persistent Disk - Block storage for Compute Engine virtual machines.
- Cloud MemoryStore - Managed in-memory data store dependent on Redis.
- Local SSD: High-execution, transient, nearby square storage.
- Filestore: High-execution record storage for Google Cloud clients.

Systems administration

- VPC - Virtual Private Cloud for dealing with the product characterized organization of cloud assets.
- Cloud Load Balancing - Software-characterized, oversaw administration for load adjusting the traffic.
- Cloud Armor - Web application firewall to shield remaining tasks at hand from DDoS assaults.

- Cloud CDN - Content Delivery Network dependent on Google's worldwide circulated edge purposes of the essence.
- Cloud Interconnect - Service to associate a server farm with Google Cloud Platform
- Cloud DNS - Managed, legitimate DNS administration running on a similar framework as Google.
- Network Service Tiers - Option to pick Premium versus Standard organization level for the higher-performing organization.

Enormous Data

- BigQuery - Scalable, oversaw venture data distribution center for analysis.
- Cloud Dataflow - Managed administration dependent on Apache Beam for stream and clump data preparation.
- Cloud Dataproc - Big data stage for running Apache Hadoop and Apache Spark occupations.
- Cloud Composer - Managed work process organization administration based on Apache Airflow.
- Cloud Datalab - Tool for data analysis, examination, representation, and AI, this is a wholly overseen Jupyter Notebook administration.
- Cloud Dataprep - Data administration dependent on Trifacta to outwardly investigate, clean, and get ready data for examination.
- Cloud Pub/Sub - Scalable occasion ingestion administration dependent on message lines.

- • Cloud Data Studio - Business knowledge instrument to imagine data through dash controls and reports.

Cloud AI

- Cloud AutoML - Service to prepare and convey custom machine learning models. As of September 2018, the administration is in Beta.
- Cloud TPU - Accelerators utilized by Google to prepare AI models.
- Cloud Machine Learning Engine - Managed administration for preparing and building AI models dependent on standard systems.
- Cloud Job Discovery - Service dependent on Google's inquiry and AI abilities for the selecting biological system.
- Dialogflow Enterprise - Development condition dependent on Google's AI for building conversational interfaces.
- Cloud Natural Language - Text examination administration dependent on Google Deep Learning models.
- Cloud Speech-to-Text - Speech to message change administration dependent on AI.
- Cloud Text-to-Speech - Text to discourse change administration dependent on AI.
- Cloud Translation API - Service to progressively interpret between a large number of accessible language sets
- Cloud Vision API - Image analysis administration dependent on AI

- Cloud Video Intelligence - Video analysis administration dependent on AI

The executive's Tools

- Stackdriver - Monitoring, logging, and diagnostics for applications on Google Cloud Platform and AWS.
- Cloud Deployment Manager - Tool to convey Google Cloud Platform assets characterized in formats made in YAML, Python, or Jinja2.
- Cloud Console - Web interface to oversee Google Cloud Platform assets.
- Cloud Shell - Browser-based shell order line admittance to oversee Google Cloud Platform assets.
- Cloud Console Mobile App - Android and iOS application to oversee Google Cloud Platform assets.
- Cloud APIs - APIs to automatically get to Google Cloud Platform assets

Character and Security

- Cloud Identity - Single sign-on (SSO) administration dependent on SAML 2.0 and OpenID.
- Cloud IAM - Identity and Access Management(IAM) administration for characterizing arrangements dependent on job-based admittance control.
- Cloud Identity-Aware Proxy - Service to control admittance to cloud applications running on Google Cloud Platform without utilizing a VPN.

- Cloud Data Loss Prevention API - Service to consequently find, characterize, and redact delicate data.
- Security Key Enforcement - Two-venture check administration dependent on a security key.
- Cloud Key Management Service - Cloud-facilitated key administration coordinated with IAM and review logging.
- Cloud Resource Manager - Service to oversee assets by the venture, envelope, and association dependent on the pecking order.
- Cloud Security Command Center - Security and data hazard stage for data and services running in Google Cloud Platform.
- Cloud Security Scanner - Automated weakness filtering administration for applications conveyed in App Engine.
- Access Transparency - Near ongoing review logs giving permeability to Google Cloud Platform managers.
- VPC Service Controls - Service to oversee security borders for touchy data in Google Cloud Platform services.

IoT

- Cloud IoT Core - Secure gadget association and the executive's administration for the Internet of Things.
- Edge TPU - Purpose-assembled ASIC intended to run deduction at the edge. As of September 2018, this item is in private Beta.
- Cloud IoT Edge - Brings AI to the edge computing layer.

Programming interface Platform

- Maps Platform - APIs for guides, courses, and places dependent on Google Maps.
- Apigee API Platform - Lifecycle the control stage to configuration, secure, convey, screen, and scale APIs.
- API Monetization - Tool for API suppliers to make income models, reports, installment passages, and designer entryway incorporations.
- Developer Portal - Self-administration stage for engineers to distribute and oversee APIs.
- API Analytics - Service to examine API-driven projects through observing, estimating, and overseeing APIs.
- Apigee Sense - Enables API security by distinguishing and making chairpersons aware of dubious API practices.
- Cloud Endpoints - A NGINX-based intermediary to send and oversee APIs.
- Service Infrastructure - A lot of basic services for building Google Cloud items.

Zones and Areas

As of Q1 2020, Google Cloud Platform is accessible in 22 areas and 61 zones[1]. A district is a particular topographical area where clients can convey cloud assets.

Every locale is an autonomous geographic zone that comprises of zones.

A zone is a sending region for Google Cloud Platform assets inside an area. Zones ought to be viewed as an isolated disappointment area inside a locale.

The vast majority of the districts have at least three zones. As of Q1 2020, Google Cloud Platform is accessible in the accompanying sections and zones:

GCP Regions & Zones

Region Name	Launch Date	Location	Zones
us-west1	Q3, 2016	The Dalles, Oregon, USA	• us-west1-a • us-west1-b • us-west1-c
us-west2	Q3, 2018	Los Angeles, California, USA	• us-west2-a • us-west2-b • us-west2-c
us-west3	Q1, 2020	Salt Lake City, Utah, USA	• us-west3-a • us-west3-b • us-west3-c
us-west4	Q2, 2020	Las Vegas, Nevada, USA	• us-west4-a • us-west4-b • us-west4-c

us-central1		Council Bluffs, Iowa, USA	• us-central1-a • us-central1-b • us-central1-c • us-central1-f
us-east1	Q4, 2015	Moncks Corner, South Carolina, USA	• us-east1-b • us-east1-c • us-east1-d
us-east4	Q2, 2017	Ashburn, Virginia, USA	• us-east4-a • us-east4-b • us-east4-c
North-America-northeast1	Q1, 2018	Montréal, Canada	• North-America-northeast1-a • North-America-northeast1-b • North-America-northeast1-c

South-America-east1	Q3, 2017	São Paulo, Brazil	• South-America-east1-a • South-America-east1-b • South-America-east1-c
europe-west2	Q2, 2017	London, U.K.	• europe-west2-a • europe-west2-b • europe-west2-c
Europe-west1		St. Ghislain, Belgium	• europe-west1-b • europe-west1-c • europe-west1-d
Europe-west4	Q1, 2018	Eemshaven, Netherlands	• Europe-west4-a • Europe-west4-b • Europe-west4-c

Europe-west6	Q1, 2019	Zurich, Switzerland	• Europe-west6-a • Europe-west6-b • Europe-west6-c
Europe-west3	Q3, 2017	Frankfurt, Germany	• europe-west3-a • europe-west3-b • europe-west3-c
europe-north1	Q2, 2018	Hamina, Finland	• europe-north1-a • europe-north1-b • europe-north1-c
Asia-south1	Q4, 2017	Mumbai, India	• asia-south1-a • asia-south1-b • asia-south1-c

Asia-southeast1	Q2, 2017	Jurong West, Singapore	• Asia-southeast1-a • Asia-southeast1-b • Asia-southeast1-c
Asia-southeast2	Q2, 2020	Jakarta, Indonesia	• Asia-southeast2-a • Asia-southeast2-b • Asia-southeast2-c • Asia-southeast2-d
Asia-east2	Q3, 2018	Hong Kong	• Asia-east2-a • Asia-east2-b • Asia-east2-c
Asia-east1		Changhua County, Taiwan	• Asia-east1-a • Asia-east1-b • Asia-east1-c
Asia-northeast1	Q4, 2016	Tokyo, Japan	• Asia-northeast1-a • Asia-northeast1-b

			• Asia-northeast1-c
Asia-northeast2	Q2, 2019	Osaka, Japan	• Asia-northeast2-a • Asia-northeast2-b • Asia-northeast2-c
Asia-northeast3	Q1, 2020	Seoul, Korea	• Asia-northeast3-a • Asia-northeast3-b • Asia-northeast3-c
Australia-southeast1	Q3, 2017	Sydney, Australia	• Australia-southeast1-a • Australia-southeast1-b • Australia-southeast1-c

The closeness to services by other cloud specialist organizations

A correlation of comparable services may help comprehend Google Cloud Platform's contributions for those acquainted with other prominent cloud specialist organizations.

Google Cloud Platform	**Amazon Web Services**[9]	**Microsoft Azure**[10]	**Oracle Cloud**[11]
Google Compute Engine	Amazon EC2	Azure Virtual Machines	Oracle Cloud Infra OCI
Google App Engine	AWS Elastic Beanstalk	Azure App Services	Oracle Application Container
Google Kubernetes Engine	Amazon Elastic Kubernetes Service	Azure Kubernetes Service	Oracle Kubernetes Service
Google Cloud Bigtable	Amazon DynamoDB	Azure Cosmos DB	Oracle NoSQL Database
Google BigQuery	Amazon Redshift	Azure Synapse Analytics	Oracle Autonomous Data Warehouse
Google Cloud Functions	AWS Lambda	Azure Functions	Oracle Cloud Fn
Google Cloud	Amazon DynamoDB	Azure Cosmos DB	Oracle NoSQL Database

Datastore

Google Cloud Storage	Amazon S3	Azure Blob Storage	Oracle Cloud Storage OCI

Certifications

Like contributions by Amazon Web Services, Microsoft Azure, and IBM Cloud, a progression of Google Cloud Certified projects are accessible on the Google Cloud Platform. Members can pick between web-based learning programs by Coursera, Pluralsight, or Qwiklabs just as live workshops and online classes. Contingent upon the program, affirmations can be earned on the web or at different testing places found worldwide.

- Associate Cloud Engineer
- Professional Data Engineer
- Professional Cloud Architect
- Professional Cloud Developer
- Professional Cloud Network Engineer
- Professional Cloud Security Engineer
- Professional Collaboration Engineer
- Professional Cloud DevOps Engineer
- G Suite

Timetable

Google Cloud Summit in 2017

- April 2008 - Google App Engine reported in a review
- May 2010 - Google Cloud Storage dispatched
- May 2010 - Google BigQuery and Prediction API reported in a review
- October 2011 - Google Cloud SQL is reported in see
- June 2012 - Google Compute Engine is sent in a review
- May 2013 - Google Compute Engine is delivered to GA
- August 2013-Cloud Storage starts consequently encoding every Storage item's data and metadata under the 128-bit Advanced Encryption Standard (AES-128), and every encryption key is itself scrambled with a usually turned arrangement of ace keys
- February 2014 - Google Cloud SQL becomes GA
- May 2014 - Google gets Stackdriver
- June 2014 - Kubernetes is declared as an open-source holder supervisor
- June 2014 - Cloud Dataflow is stated in a review
- October 2014 - Google gets Firebase
- November 2014 - Alpha delivery Google Kubernetes Engine (previously Container Engine) is reported

- January 2015 - Google Cloud Monitoring dependent on Stackdriver goes into Beta
- March 2015 - Google Cloud Pub/Sub opens up in Beta
- April 2015 - Google Cloud DNS turns out to be commonly accessible
- April 2015 - Google Dataflow dispatched in Beta
- July 2015 - Google discharges v1 of Kubernetes; Hands it over to The Cloud Native Computing Foundation
- August 2015 - Google Cloud Dataflow, Google Cloud Pub/Sub, Google Kubernetes Engine, and Deployment Manager graduate to GA
- November 2015 - Bebop is gained, and Diane Greene joins Google
- February 2016 - Google Cloud Functions opens up in Alpha
- September 2016 - Apigee, a supplier of use programming interface (API) the executive's organization, is gained by Google
- September 2016 - Stackdriver turns out to be commonly accessible
- February 2017 - Cloud Spanner, a profoundly accessible, internationally conveyed database, is delivered into Beta
- March 2017 - Google gains Kaggle, the world's biggest network of data researchers and AI aficionados
- April 2017 - MIT teacher Andrew Sutherland breaks the

record for the biggest Compute Engine bunch with 220,000 centers on Preemptible VMs.

- May 2017 - Google Cloud IoT Core is dispatched in Beta
- November 2017 - Google Kubernetes Engine gets ensured by the CNCF
- February 2018 - Google Cloud IoT Core turns out to be commonly accessible
- February 2018 - Google reports its purpose to obtain Xively
- February 2018 - Cloud TPUs, ML quickening agents for Tensorflow, become available in Beta May 2018 - Gartner names Google as a Leader in the 2018 Gartner Infrastructure as Service Magic Quadrant
- May 2018 - Google Cloud Memorystore opens up in Beta
- April 2019 - Google Cloud Run (ultimately oversaw) Beta delivery
- April 2019 - Google Anthos declared
- November 2019 - Google Cloud Run (eventually managed) General accessibility discharge
- March 2020 - Due to the COVID-19 pandemic, Google Cloud delayed the web-based streaming rendition of its Google Cloud Next uber gathering, fourteen days after it dropped the in-person form.

Who is a Google Professional Data Engineer?

Proficient Data Engineer

A Professional Data Engineer empowers data-driven dynamic by gathering, changing, and distributing data. A Data Engineer ought to have the option to configuration, fabricate, operationalize, secure, and screen data handling systems with specific accentuation on security and consistency, adaptability and effectiveness, unwavering quality and devotion, and adapt movability. A Data Engineer ought to likewise have the option to use, send, and persistently train previous AI models.

The Professional Data Engineer test evaluates your capacity to:

- Design data preparing systems
- Build and operationalize data preparing systems
- Operationalize AI models
- Ensure arrangement quality

CHAPTER TWO - DESIGN DATA PROCESSING SYSTEMS

Data Processing systems

For the most part, "the collecting and control of data to create significant data." In this sense, it very well may be viewed as a subset of data preparing, "the change (handling) of data in any way perceivable by an onlooker."

The term Data Processing (DP) has also been utilized to allude to a division inside an association liable for data handling applications' activity.

Data Processing Functions

Data handling may include different cycles, including:

- Validation – Ensuring that the provided data is right and essential.
- Sorting – "organizing things in some succession and uninterested sets."
- Summarization – diminishing actual data to its primary concerns.
- Aggregation – consolidating various bits of data.
- Analysis – the "assortment, association, examination, translation and introduction of data."

- Reporting – list detail or outline data or registered data.
- Classification – partition of data into different classes.

Data handling framework

A data handling framework is a mix of machines, individuals, and cycles that, for many data sources, create a characterized set of yields. The source of data and outputs is deciphered as data, realities, data, and so forth, relying upon the mediator's connection to the framework.

A term ordinarily utilized equivalently with a data handling framework is a data framework. Concerning electronic data handling, the relating idea is alluded to as an electronic data preparation framework.

A data handling framework may include a blend of:

- Conversion is changing over data to another structure or Language.
- Validation – Ensuring that provided data is "spotless, right, and valuable."
- Sorting – "organizing things in some succession and various sets."
- Summarization – diminishing subtlety data to its primary concerns.
- Aggregation – consolidating numerous bits of data.
- Analysis – the "assortment, association, examination, translation, and introduction of data.".
- Reporting – list detail or synopsis data or processed data.

The principal machines utilized for data handling were punched card machines; presently, PCs are being used.

Sorts of data preparing systems

By application region

Logical data handling

Logical data handling "ordinarily includes a lot of calculation (number-crunching and examination activities) upon a moderately limited quantity of data, bringing about a little volume of yield."

Business data handling

Business data handling "includes an enormous volume of info data, generally barely any computational activities, and a huge volume of yield." Accounting programs are prototypical instances of data preparing applications. Data Systems (IS) is the field that reviews, for example, hierarchical PC systems.

Data examination

"Data examination is a collection of strategies that help to portray realities, recognize designs, create clarifications, and test hypotheses."] For instance, data analysis may be utilized to take a gander at deals and client data to "distinguish associations between items to consider strategically pitching efforts."

By administration type

- Transaction preparing systems
- Data storage and recovery systems
- Command and control systems

- Computing administration systems
- Process control systems
- Message exchanging systems

Models

Basic model

An elementary case of a data preparing framework is the way toward keeping up a check register. Exchanges—checks and stores—are recorded as they happen, and the exchanges are summed up to decide a current parity. Month to month, the register's data is accommodated with an ideally indistinguishable rundown of exchanges prepared by the bank.

A more advanced record-keeping framework may also recognize the exchanges, such as stores by source or checks by type, such as altruistic commitments. This data may be utilized to acquire data like all out of all obligations for the year.

The significant thing about this model is that it is a framework where all exchanges are recorded reliably, and a similar strategy for bank compromise is utilized each time.

Genuine model

It is a flowchart of a data processing system combining manual and computerized processing to handle accounts receivable, billing, and general ledger

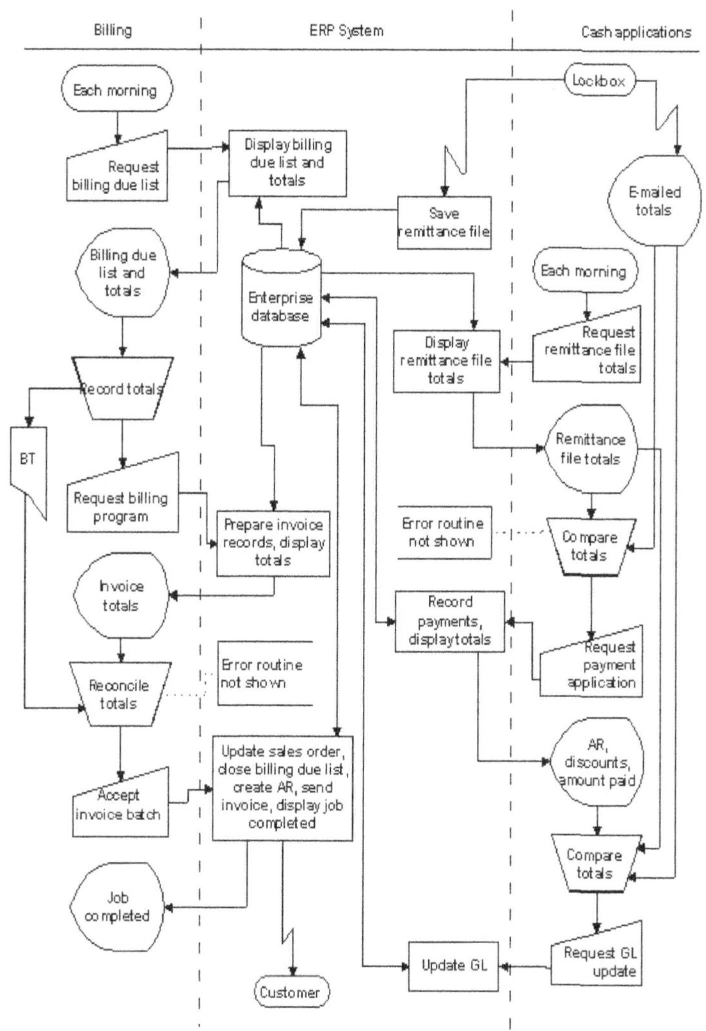
Billing
ERP System
Cash applications
Each morning
Request billing due list
Display billing due list and totals
Lockbox
Save remittance file
E-mailed totals
Billing due list and totals
Enterprise database
Each morning
Display remittance file totals
Request remittance file totals
Record totals
BT
Remittance file totals
Request billing program
Prepare invoice records, display totals
Error routine not shown
Compare totals
Invoice totals
Record payments, display totals
Request payment application
Reconcile totals
Error routine not shown
Update sales order, close billing due list, create AR, send invoice, display job completed
AR, discounts, amount paid
Accept invoice batch
Compare totals
Job completed
Update GL
Request GL update
Customer

Various Types

There are three kinds of data preparing, they are

Manual Data Processing

The data prepared physically by human activities without utilizing any device is manual handling. For instance, physically composing or ascertaining a report physically and precisely is a manual handling, physically confirming imprints sheet, budgetary count, and so forth. The principle drawback is that manual preparation requires high work costs, high time utilization, more mistakes, and so on. Thus with this hindrance, more development tools have come where handling work is done consequently.

Electronic Data Processing (EDP)

It is likewise called as data services or systems. It measures the crude data through PCs and projects utilizing electronic correspondence; the preparing work is swift. The best electronic data preparation model is an ATM card, which is implanted with an electronic chip.

Ongoing Data Processing

It is a constant cycle, which reacts inside seconds when the data input is given; it gets handled and provides wanted yield data. For instance, an individual needs to draw a specific sum from his record utilizing an ATM. When he embeds the card and enters balance, he needs to pull alongside the ATM pin; the machine measures the exchange and refreshed his ledger balance online inside a couple of moments. The principle advantage is time utilization.

Data Processing Cycle

This handling cycle is normal for both manual and electronic preparation. It is the arrangement of steps for extricating data from crude data. There are three significant stages in this preparing they are,

Info

The cycle through which data gathered is changed into a structure that the PC can comprehend. It is the most significant advance because the right yield results rely upon the given data. The exercises completed in data input are of four phases; they are

- Data Collection
- Data Encoding
- Data Transmission
- Data Communication

Data Collection

Data assortment is a significant advance in preparing where all crude realities are gathered from different situations, which ought to be very much characterized and exact to measures it. Instances of data assortment are land reviews, political decision surveying.

Data Encoding

Changing over crude realities into a more straightforward structure to contribute to the preparing framework is data encoding.

Data Transmission

At this stage, the data is sent to the processor and different segments of the framework

Data Communication

At this stage, the data is imparted between different preparing systems.

Cycle

This stage-manages controlling crude data are utilizing different tools or programming strategies to significant data. Numerous product instruments are accessible to handle enormous volumes of data inside a brief period. It very well may be clarified in basic structure in the accompanying case of a computerization data handling strategy; the client composes a program to perform expansion of two numbers, which contains a set of directions; this program is prepared for the focal handling unit, which measures data dependent on the guidance given. Presently the product controls the data, which provides directions to deal with data and gives important anticipated data.

data preparing model

There are three unique sorts of data controlling methods they are

- Classification: Data has isolated in like manner into various gatherings and subgroups at this stage to achieve anything but challenging to measure.
- Storing: At this stage, data is put away in an appropriate arrangement, so it tends to be handily gotten to when required.
- Calculation: At this stage, a few tasks are performed on the data to create wanted outcomes.

Yield

At this stage, the data yield, which is acquired after handling, is significant data that is required for end-clients. The result can be obtained in various structures like sound, video, report print, etc. Coming up next are the exercises done in out they are,

- Decoding: The data which is encoded is decoded into the getting design.
- Communication: The yield created is dispersed to different areas so any client can get to it whenever.
- Retrieval: Anyone at one's feelings can get to the data that is appropriated and put away.

Capacity Stage

The handled data is put away in virtual data memory for additional utilization; it is a significant phase of the cycle since we can recover the data when required.

Data Processing in Research Area

The significant advances principally remember for this handling are as per the following,

1. Questionnaire checking
2. Editing
3. Coding
4. Classification
5. Tabulation
6. Graphical Representation
7. Data Cleaning
8. Data Adjustment

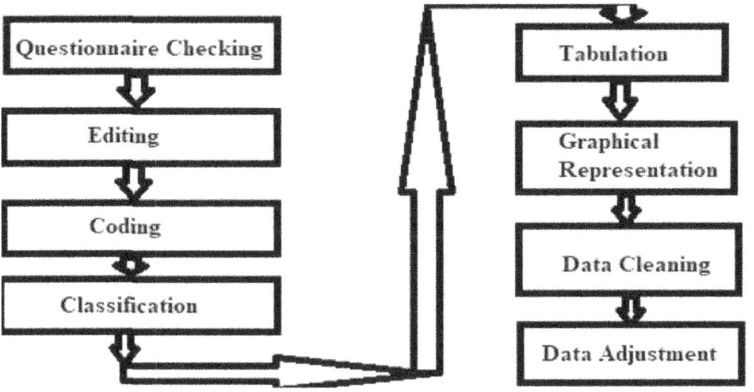

data-processing-in-research-area, photo credit: elprocus.com

- Questionnaire checking: The initial step is to check if there are any surveys or no. Not many of not satisfactory polls are deficient or halfway data, insufficient data.

- Editing data is recognized if there are any mistakes in crude data so that on the off chance that they are blunders, they can be altered and adjusted.

- Coding is the way toward giving images so that reactions can be put into their separate gatherings.

- Classification of data depends on a class stretch, recurrence, or qualities like the city and the populace.

- After grouping, we classify the whole cycle in various significant sections and columns.

- Then speak to them in graphical or factual bar outline design.

- After that, we check the whole data indeed from first if there is any absent

Data we include it up for consistency.

- An extra idea of data altering is done as corresponding to improve quality.

Points of interest

The upsides of data handling are

- Highly proficient
- Time-sparing
- High speed
- Reduces mistakes

Hindrances

The hindrances of data handling are

- Large power utilization
- Occupies enormous memory
- The cost of establishment is high
- Wastage of memory.

Applications

The utilization of data handling is

- In the financial segment, this preparation is utilized by the bank clients to check there, bank subtleties, exchange, and different subtleties.

- In instructive offices like schools and universities, this handling is appropriate for discovering understudy subtleties like biodata, class, move number, marks acquired, etc.
- In the exchange cycle, the application refreshes the data when clients demand their subtleties.
- In the following calculated region, this handling helps in recovering the necessary client data on the web.
- In clinics, patients, subtleties can be handily looked at.

Designing Data Processing Systems

Designing data processing systems incorporates planning adaptable data portrayals, planning data pipelines, and planning data preparing the infrastructure. You will see that these three things appear in the test's initial segment with comparable but not indistinguishable contemplations. Similar inquiries or intrigue appear in changed settings, data portrayal, pipelines, handling framework. For instance, developments in technology could make the data portrayal of a picked arrangement obsolete. The data preparing pipeline may have been executed in an extremely included change now accessible as a solitary effective order, and administration could supplant the framework more attractive characteristics. Nonetheless, as you'll see, there are extra worries with each part. For instance, framework accessibility is critical to pipeline preparation, however not data portrayal, and the limit is essential to handling, yet not the theoretical pipeline or the portrayal. Consider data designing and Google Cloud as a stage comprising of parts that can be gathered into arrangements. We should audit the components of GCP that structure the data building stage. Capacity and databases, benefits that empower putting away and recovering data, and diverse capacity and recovery techniques make them more effective for clear use cases. Worker based handling benefits that empower application code and programming to run that can utilize put away data to perform activities, activities, and changes creating results. Incorporated services, joined capacity, and adaptable preparing in a structure intended to handle data instead of general applications, more productive and adaptable than disconnected worker database arrangements. Human-made reasoning helps distinguish, tag, arrange, and foresee three hard or difficult activities to achieve in data handling without AI. Pre and post-preparing services, working with data and pipelines before handling, for example, data cleanup or in the wake of handling, for example, data representation. Pre and post-preparing are significant pieces of a data handling arrangement. Foundation benefits, all the system benefits that associate and coordinate data preparing and IT components into a total arrangement. Informing, systems, data import, send out, security, observing, etc. Capacity and database systems are planned and streamlined for putting away and recovering. They are not worked to do data change. It's accepted in their plan that the registering power important to perform changes on the data is outside of the capacity or data set. The association strategy and access technique for every one of these services are proficient for clear cases. For instance, a Cloud SQL database is truly adept at putting away predictable individual exchanges. Yet, it's not advanced for putting away a lot of unstructured data like video records. Database services perform a minor procedure on the data inside the entrance technique; for instance, SQL inquiries can total, amass, tally, and sum up an inquiry question's after-effects. Here's a test tip, know the contrasts between Cloud SQL and Cloud Spanner and when to utilize each. Administration differentiators incorporate access strategies, the expense of speed of explicit activities, sizes of data, and how data is sorted out and put away. Subtleties and contrasts between the data developments are examined later in this course. A test tip, realize how to recognize developments in reverse from their properties. For instance, which data technology offers the quickest ingestive data? Which one may you use for ingestive streaming data? Overseen services are ones where you can see the particular occasion or bunch. Test tip oversaw benefits have some IT overhead. It doesn't dispose of the overhead or manual strategies, yet it limits them contrasted and on-prem arrangements. Serverless services eliminate a greater amount of IT duty, so dealing with the basic workers isn't essential for your overhead, and the individual examples are not obvious. Later expansion to this rundown is Cloud Firestore. Cloud Firestore is a NoSQL report database that worked for programmed scaling. It offers superior and simplicity of use development, and it incorporates a data store similarity mode. As referenced, storage and databases give limited handling capacities, and what they do offer is with regards to look and recovery. Yet, you'll need data handling programming and computing power on the off chance that you have to perform more modern activities and changes on the data. So, where do you get these assets? You could utilize any of these processing stages to composing your application or parts of an application to store your database services. You could introduce open-source programming, for example, MySQL, an open-source database, or Hadoop, an open-source data preparation stage on Compute Engine. Fabricate your-own answers are driven generally by business prerequisites. They, for the most part, include more IT overhead than utilizing a Cloud stage administration. These three data preparing services include in pretty much every data designing arrangement. Each covers with the other, implying that some work could be refined in either a few of these services. Progressed arrangements may utilize one, two, or each of the three. Data preparing services to join storage and figure and mechanize the capacity and register parts of data handling through reflections. For instance, in Cloud Dataproc, Spark's data reflection is a tough circulated dataset or RDD, and the preparing deliberation is a coordinated non-cyclic chart, DAG. In BigQuery, the reflections are table and question, and in Dataflow, the deliberations are PCollection and pipeline. Actualizing storage and handling as reflections empower the entire systems to adjust to the tremendous burden. The client data architect to zero in on the data and business issues they're attempting to fathom. There's incredible likely worth and item or cycle development utilizing AI. AI can take unstructured data, for example, logs helpful by distinguishing or sorting the data and empowering business insight. Perceiving an example of something that exists is firmly identified with foreseeing a future occasion dependent on experience. AI is utilized for distinguishing, ordering, and anticipating. It can make unstructured data valuable. Your test tip is to comprehend the variety of AI developments offered on TCP and when you should utilize each. A data designing arrangement includes data ingest, control during preparation, analysis, and perception. These components can be basic to business necessities. Here are a couple of services that you ought to be commonly acquainted with. Data move services work on the web, and data move tools are a shippable gadget utilized for synchronizing data in the Cloud with an external source. Cloud Data Studio is utilized for the representation of data after it has been handled. Cloud Dataprep is utilized to plan or condition data and to get ready pipelines before handling data. Cloud Datalab is a scratch pad that is an independent workspace that holds code, executes the code, and shows results. Dialogflow is help for making chatbots. It utilizes AI to give a strategy to coordinate human communication with data. Your test tip here is to acquaint yourself with infrastructure benefits that show up generally in data building arrangements. Frequently they're utilized on account of key highlights they give. For instance, Cloud Pub/Sub can hold a directive for as long as seven days giving versatility to data building arrangements that, in any case, would be extremely hard to execute. Each help in the Google Cloud stage could be utilized in a data designing arrangement. Nonetheless, the absolute generally normal and significant services have appeared here. Cloud Pub/Sub, and informing administration, includes in practically all live or streaming data arrangements since it decouples data appearance from data ingests. Cloud VPN, Partner Interconnect, or Dedicated Interconnect, assume a job at whatever point there's data on-premise, it must be communicated to services in the Cloud. Cloud IAM, firewall rules, and key administration are basic to certain verticals, such as medical care and budgetary ventures. Each arrangement should be observed and overseen, which generally includes controls showed in Cloud Console and data sent to Stackdriver checking. It's smart to analyze test arrangements that utilize data handling or data building advances and focus on the arrangement's infrastructure parts. It's imperative to comprehend what the services add to the data arrangements and be acquainted with key highlights and alternatives. There is a lot of subtitles that I wouldn't remember; for instance, the specific number of IAP upheld by a particular occasion is something I would hope to turn upward and not know. Likewise, the expense of a specific case type contrasted and another occasion type, the genuine qualities, isn't something I would expect I'd have to know as a data engineer.

Nonetheless, the way that an implement standard example has higher IAPs than an N1 standard occasion, or that the N4 typical cost over an N1 standard, are ideas that I would need to know as a data engineer

Data Design Patterns

The act of Design Patterns is generally mainstream in Object-Oriented Programming (OOP), which has been adequately clarified and summed up in the exemplary book "Plan Patterns: Elements of Reusable Object-Oriented Software" by Erich Gamma and Richard Helm.

Coming up next is the importance of the Design Pattern from Wikipedia: "A programming configuration design is a general, reusable answer for a regularly happening issue inside a given setting in programming plan. It's anything but a completed plan that can be changed straightforwardly into the source or machine code. It is a portrayal or format for tackling a difficult that can be utilized in various circumstances. Configuration designs are formalized accepted procedures that the developer can use to take care of basic issues when planning an application or framework."

Numerous individuals may have posed a similar inquiry for information science: does information science programming have configuration designs? I would state, yes. Notwithstanding, to separate them from OOP, I would call them Design Principles for information science, which implies equivalent to Design Patterns for OOP, yet at a somewhat more elevated level. As motivated by Robert Martin's book "Clean Architecture," this article centers around 4 top plan standards for information handling and information designing. My next article will be on basic plan standards for advanced execution. In the two regions, there are reusable arrangements and best practices that have been demonstrated to:

1. Reduce the general development cycle;
2. Make the data cycle simpler to keep up (regardless of which programming language or data planning device is utilized);
3. Make the framework more open and straightforward to work;
4. Ensure data quality from the earliest starting point.

Plan Principle 1: Always Start with Design of Datasets and Data Entities

Each data cycle has three insignificant segments: Input Data, Output Data, and data changes in the middle. At whatever point planning a data cycle, the principal thing that ought to be done is to characterize the data dataset(s), just as the yield dataset, including:

- The input data collections and reference data required
- The yield dataset to be made
- The data fields in each of the datasets
- The data kind of each field, for example, text, whole number, skim, list, and so forth.,
- The fields that decide the uniqueness of each record
- The expected data example of each field, including whether it can have missing qualities and a particular rundown of qualities
- The relationship of the datasets with other existing datasets in the association

It is like the purported Data Modeling applied to the database and, at times, alluded to as a "legitimate data set plan." The catchphrase here is "sensible" because it ought to occur before execution choices. A dataset could be composed to circle and put away inside the organization and be the natural resource to go to or utilized by different cycles and applications in the long run. Therefore, it is significant and ought to be precisely and characterized, with the accepted procedures and strategies driven by Data Governance. A yield dataset should be described precisely depending on business prerequisites or required by the downstream segments or cycles. A data set should be reliably described with its source so the data genealogy can be effectively followed across various systems.

After the consistent plan, the physical area and data structure for a given dataset would then be resolved as a feature of the framework plan. It regularly happens that the physical structure cannot be the same as legitimate plans. A commonplace model is that a field name in the coherent strategy ought to have specific words to make it more significant and decipherable. In contrast, the physical field name needs to consider the framework or programming restriction. For instance:

- Logical Field Name: Employee Name
- Physical Field Name (can't have space, and has an impediment on the number of characters): emp_nm

When the data stage in an association is changed, the intelligent definitions ought not to change. Simultaneously, the physical portrayal of a dataset can be upgraded depending on the framework's necessities and capacities.

On the off chance that a cycle stream requires numerous means, the substance of the transitional datasets should also be characterized, which can fill various needs:

- For data quality checking
- Providing measure checkpoints and stages, with the end goal that the cycle doesn't have to consistently re-run from the earliest starting point when it falls flat
- Act as the contribution for another sub-processor usable by different systems or clients

As contrasted and the code for data measure rationale, a data element requires more prolonged and more exertion to change with more extensive effect, principally because it holds the data and could be utilized by different cycles. When info, middle of the road, and yield datasets are characterized, the data cycle's skeleton is set up. We frequently observe data engineers begin constructing the cycle without unmistakably characterizing the yield; first, this could undoubtedly prompt two outcomes: 1) more significant changes or even a patch up of the process when the product is changed; 2) have the yield rely upon the preparing rationale, consequently, miss a portion of the prerequisites or be poorly characterized. So consistently start with describing the datasets before you begin to plan the specialized cycle. To a great extent, the preparing rationale relies upon the data meanings of the info and yield at any rate.

The datasets and data substances' consistent plan is also firmly connected with the underlying industry necessity gathering, data disclosure, and data administration cycle to keep the association guidelines. The cautious coherent plan should also consider data sharing inside an association, evading copy datasets if a field or data has existed elsewhere in the organization (see my article: Master Data Management: An Essential Part of Data Strategy). Ultimately, a clear rationale plan of data collections with excellent administration is a basic advance to guarantee data quality from the earliest starting point (see my article: 7 Steps to Ensure and Sustain Data Quality).

Plan Principle 2: Separate Business Rules from Processing Logic

In Robert Martin's "Perfect Architecture" book, one of the standards is to isolate Business Rules from Plugins, from the product point of view and precisely the OOP capacities. In Data designing, in any case, comparable standards exist, while the business rules have a lot more extensive ramifications. Above all else, business rules comprise various sorts, such as explicit philosophies in Marketing, Finance, Security, or Compliance. Much of the time, the guidelines for data purging and normalization can be additionally determined by business divisions and, along these lines, be considered business rules. Business Rules regularly have three qualities:

1. Need to be assessed by business associations or business investigators

2. Could be changed periodically and require a brisk turnaround
3. Lead to basic effect and results if they are not designed or executed effectively

The administration and execution of business rules are basic for the achievement of a data processor. A proper structure should consider the following:

1. Modularization

Similar rules ought to be taken care of in an identical data cycle, module, or capacity. Then again, various sorts of regulations should not live in a similar cycle, module, or ability. Else, it gets hard to deal with the effect of changes in business rules, and the process turns out to be a lot harder to keep up.

How about we take a little case of preparing a bit of client review data, where you have to clean the crude data, normalize it, and afterward load the normalized data into a data set table. Here the yield is the standard database table, and your overview data is the crude info. There are two different ways of building the cycle:

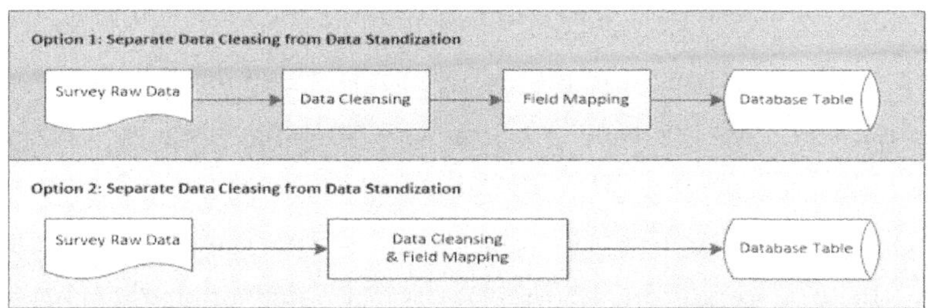

Data purifying standards are not quite the same as those for field planning: data purging principles depend on the estimations of info data, while field planning depends on the data structures of both info and yield. Given this, an alternative one is better since it permits data purifying guidelines to be changed freely from field planning, consequently prompting greater adaptability and effortlessness, just as less effect for rule alterations when contrasted with choice 2. As such, away from various kinds of rules drives better administration of the principles with negligible impact on different sorts of rules just as another preparing rationale. Additionally, the unique capacity or module zeroing in on one kind of business rules can be developed as autonomous assistance when required. It would then be able to be effectively changed or improved independently for other use cases.

2. Metadata Storage of Business Rules

At whatever point conceivable, the business's aspect that is changed regularly ought to be preoccupied out and put away in an archive (e.g., a database), separate from the programming code itself. With this detachment set up, an application or API would then be based on its head, through which business examiners and business clients can survey and adjust the business rules. On the handling side, the motor peruses the guidelines from the archive at the execution time. It applies the principles to the data with no business rationale hard-coded into the cycle itself.

3. Business Rules Versioning and Logging

After the business rules are put away and overseen independently in a meta-data archive, further forming and logging capacity becomes incredibly ground-breaking to empower clients to change the guidelines in another variant and contrast the outcomes of those from the past rendition, before favoring or delivering the changes. Additionally, logging the products when per business rule is fundamental to controlling the precision of the guidelines' execution and guarantee the nature of the yield data made from the standards motor.

Plan Principle 3: Build Exceptions from the earliest starting point

Data can never be significant; subsequently, we will never accept the data is flawless in any case. Data exemption handlings, for example, the accompanying, ought to be considered in the underlying plan:

- Does the dataset have a normal arrangement?
- Does the data dataset have the correct number of records, or is it unfilled? Many programming dialects don't fizzle if a document is vacant — necessities to catch the unfilled record special case unequivocally.
- Does every segment have the correct data type? Once more, a few projects can bomb quietly when barely any qualities in a portion of the records have an inappropriate arrangement.
- Define the conditions when a particular case ought to be raised: 1) Should there be a notice while the cycle can proceed, or should the cycle fizzle; 2) Who will be the beneficiaries accepting the caution?

Dealing with exceptional data cases is basic to guarantee data quality in any case. A very much planned cycle ought to have every one of these exemptions pre-characterized and, in this manner, caught simultaneously. The exemptions can prompt ongoing cautions and be taken into incorporated data quality reports and dash controls.

Plan Principle 4: Easy to Integrate utilizing Standard Input and Output

How might we make a data cycle simple to coordinate? One significant rule is to make normalized input and normalized yield layers to "epitomize" the principle cycle. As represented in the graph underneath, the cycle to normalize the data should be isolated and decoupled from the principle process. Its yield is the standard info dataset for the primary cycle. Later on, if there is one more kind of info data, a different normalization cycle can be constructed and coordinated, without changing the primary process, and this additionally applied for the yield when conceivably various configurations of result should be produced, a standard yield layer ought to be created; first, this permits future results to be delivered from the standard output by building a different cycle, without expecting to change the fundamental cycle. The standard data and yield datasets act at the association point, with the end goal that different cycles can be effectively coordinated with the primary process.

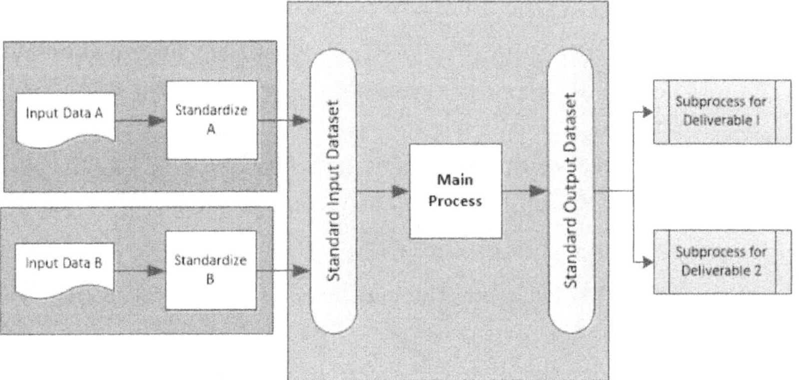

Conclusions

This article sums up four plan standards of data preparation and building. These standards should not exclusively be utilized to plan enormous systems by data designers yet also used on littler cycles by data researchers and data engineers. On the off chance that these standards are embraced in a restrained manner, and all-around planned data cycle will make it a lot simpler to keep up, more useful to be changed with less effect on different pieces of the framework, and ultimately convey preferable data quality over those that don't follow the above standards.

Building and Maintaining Data Pipelines

The following segment is on building and looking after pipelines. We've just secured a ton of this data in the plan area. Apache Beam is an open programming stage for bringing together clump and streaming. Before Apache Beam, you required two pipelines to adjust inertness, throughput, and adaptation to internal failure. Cloud Dataflow is Apache Beam as assistance. This completely overseen auto-scaling administration runs Beam pipelines. Ceaseless data can show up faulty. Basic windowing can isolate related occasions into autonomous windows. They are losing relationship data, time-sensitive windowing, or rearranging defeats this restriction. Cloud Dataflow assets are conveyed on-request per work, and work is continually rebalanced across assets. Cloud Dataflow fathoms many stream handling issues, remembering changes for size, spikes, and development after some time. It can scale while remaining flaw open-minded. It has an adaptable programming model and strategies to work with data showing up after the expected time or faulty. All data preparing is behind or slacks occasions because of idleness and the conveyance of the occasion message. Windowing is too cluttered to even think about explaining here, and I simply need to feature that you may need to know it, so ensure you get it. There is no substitution for the Dataflow Windowing ability for streaming data. Windowing makes singular outcomes for various cuts of occasion time. Windowing splits a pinnacle assortment into limited pieces dependent on each message's occasion season. It very well may be valuable in numerous specific circumstances, yet it's necessary while collecting over interminable data. Do you know the essential windowing techniques, including fixed time, such as an everyday window, sliding, and covering windows, for example, the most recent 24 hours and meeting-based windows set off to catch explosions of movement? Make sure to contemplate side sources of info. On the off chance that you comprehend side sources of information, you'll nearly understand numerous reliant ideas important for Cloud Dataflow.

MODEL OPS

Similarly, as you wouldn't prepare competitors and not have them contend, the equivalent can be said about data science and AI (ML). You wouldn't invest this energy and cash on making ML models without placing them into creation, okay? You need your models implanted into the business so they can help settle on urgent choices.

Model Operations, or Model Ops, is the appropriate response. Model Ops is the cycle of operationalizing data science by getting data science models into the creation and afterward overseeing them. The four primary strides in the Model Ops measure, design, manage, launch/incorporate, and monitor structure a repeatable cycle that you can use to reuse your models as programming relics. Model Ops (otherwise known as ML Ops) guarantees that models keep conveying an association's incentive. They also give basic experiences to deal with the expected dangers of model-based dynamic, even as basic business and specialized conditions change.

Model Ops is a cross-utilitarian, cooperative, continuous cycle that centers around overseeing AI models to make them reusable and exceptionally accessible through a repeatable organization measure. Furthermore, Model Ops includes different administration angles, for example, model forming, examining, checking, and reviving to guarantee they are as yet conveying positive business esteem as conditions change.

Associations need to comprehensively understand data science and AI models' estimation instead of essentially a cycle of creating models. At the same time, data science and ML measures are centered around building models, Model Ops centers around operationalizing the whole data science pipeline inside a business framework. Model Ops requires the arrangement and coordination of various personas inside an association, including data engineers, data researchers, business clients, IT activities, and application designers.

Numerous associations have a devoted Model Ops Engineer to encourage this cycle. ML models that are human confronting must be unbiased, reasonable, and logical; that is what the public requests and administrative organizations and bodies progressively require. For such applications, the ML Ops lifecycle must be intended to empower straightforwardness and logic regarding different dangers.

THE FOUR-STEP APPROACH TO MODEL OPS

To unravel regular trouble spots regarding display operationalization —, for example, the long postponement between starting a data science venture and conveying the model — organizations adopt a four-venture strategy: manufacture, oversee, send/incorporate, and screen.

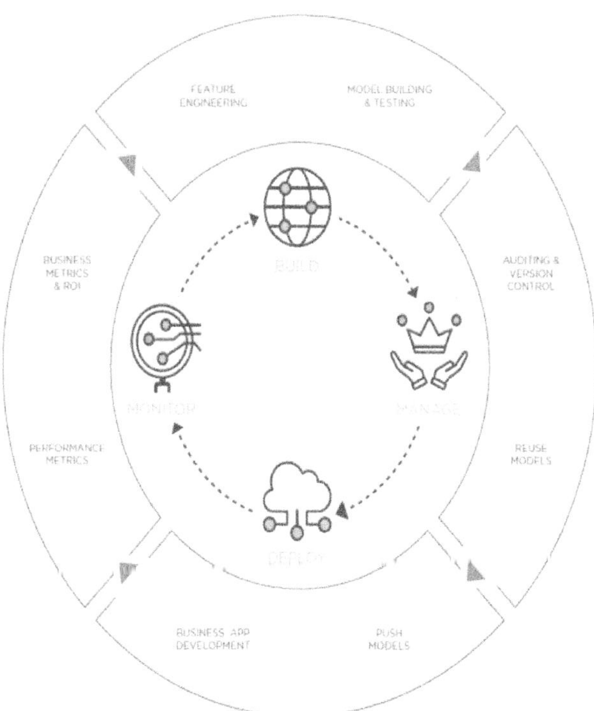

Build

Data researchers use dialects like Python and R, just as business applications, to make examination pipelines. They utilize imaginative ML calculations, manufacture prescient models, and engineer new highlights that better speak to the business issue and lift the model's prescient intensity. When building prescient models, data researchers need to consider both how the data is organized situations underway. Likewise, data researchers need to ensure that any new highlights can be made quickly enough continuously creation situations for include building.

Manage

Models have a day to day existence cycle that is best overseen from a focal storehouse where their provenance, forming, endorsement, testing, arrangement, and inevitable substitution can be followed. Other than the metadata related to model curious, the administration stage and the vault should follow exactness measurements just as conditions among models and data collections.

Deploy/Integrate

A data science pipeline is taken from its unique development condition and communicated in a structure that can be executed autonomously and incorporated into business applications. Finally, you should have the option to send the pipeline in a configuration/language proper to the objective runtime condition.

Monitor

After a model has been conveyed, it is checked for the precision of its forecasts and effect on the business. The model needs to stay exact, even as the basic data changes. This considers contribution from a human master or, consequently, through continuous retraining and champion-challenger circles with a human's endorsement.

Understand the estimation of data science through Model Ops

By using this four-venture approach, associations can understand the estimation of data science through Model Ops. It guarantees that the best model gets installed into a business framework and that the model stays current. Furthermore, organizations that train this have a major upper hand over those that reliably neglect to operationalize models and neglect to organize activity over simple knowledge. Associations can move past only structure models to operationalizing their data science utilization

Settling on viable choices over a venture, an administration, or a planet includes utilizing all around planned programming to investigate data. To operationalize data-driven reasoning, you need a choice domain that can be imitated reliably, in numerous circumstances.

Most associations come up short at this since they essentially don't have a choice approach set up. Choices are "simply made," and things occur thus. Do partners ponder the viability of that choice? Or on the other hand, are the variables that prompted a choice, and its outcome, covered in intricacy?

To do this, organizations need to build up a repeatable and straightforward cycle for choosing, a best practice for choosing: a system that works in any circumstance, and that permits partners to ponder and gain from the choices they make.

Five Steps Toward Operationalization

Significantly, the system ought not to need IT assets to execute and should cover five key stages:

1. Systematize the choice cycle and area ability so both can be handily inspected, rehashed, and shared. Codification is the basic initial phase in making both a bit of data or rationale review trail for all choice

rationale, which can rise above people and associations. When recorded, the choice rationale can be shared, improved, refreshed, examined, tried, and reproduced. Maybe similarly significant, choice rationale arranged as a business cycle can be actualized reliably through an undertaking and with any end-client.

2. Record the choice and the variables and data that prompted it. Numerous business choices, client connections, or medicines are administered by guidelines and must stay agreeable to lawful or business best practices. By catching both choice rationale, just as the data and examination that educated a business choice or cycle, a venture can make an auditable paper trail that suffers as people or data laborers travel every which way. As individuals proceed onward to new undertakings, an endeavor data or choice administration arrangement can catch and report the subtleties that would somehow or another be lost with the first donors.

3. Model the analysis used to decide, with models that can be overseen and re-purposed. Part of the test with the ascent of progressively serious examination and data science practice is the capacity to use best practices over an association. Making prescient systematic calculations isn't sufficient. Having the option to share best practices and make cross-hierarchical joint effort gives chances to productively scale the utilization and intensity of analysis all through a venture. Likewise, making all the more remarkable analysis and choice cycle by associating, in any case, different pieces of associations progressively improve an associations capacity to interface with, and dazzle, clients (i.e., interfacing new client controlling with client lifecycle showcasing, misrepresentation identification, upsell advertising, and so forth.).

4. Enhance the models as business conditions and data change to guarantee they convey the outcomes you need. Enhancement of the choice robotization measure gives two unmistakable and outstanding

chances:

- First, an opportunity to calibrate choices, offers, or medicines to more readily line up with business needs.
- Second, the capacity to mimic the progressions or adjustments of the dynamic cycle, new examination, or new data on client associations or choices.

Just including examination or classifying business rules to a business cycle doesn't associate either to a business' needs; this is the worth that enhancement gives: articulating, reenacting, and conveying choices in a way that keeps an association adjusted and on target.

5. Adjust models so they can be applied to different choice situations. Improve choices by estimating results, assessing victories (counting the utilization of champion/challenger testing to analyze acknowledged cycles against choices), and enhancing further. Picking up, adjusting, and advancing examination is the thing that AI and human-made consciousness are about; what it suggests is that the more you learn, the better you get at foreseeing or illuminating a dynamic cycle.

Whether this is done physically or expressly, it is the distinction between a conventional learning circle and human-made reasoning. The worth is in robotizing and refining improvement. Utilizing technology and expository calculations to see drifts that may not be self-evident, improve results quicker, make associations that would make some way or another imperceptible, and influence data to be more deft, agile, and proficient.

With this choice technique set up, associations can improve their choices, and more individuals can draw in at essential focuses in the choosing cycle.

The product is willing. It's not important to fabricate a domain like this exclusively without any preparation. (Actually, endeavoring to do so would be cumbersome.) Groundbreaking choice demonstrating and the control arrangements, which are heaps of examination experience, are ideal for supporting an organized, repeatable cycle for choosing. These arrangements are rising now to some degree since they can be conveyed from the cloud. This makes enormous assets any organization's removal, regardless of their size or the degree of its on-premises IT venture.

Utilizing these product arrangements and a thorough approach, leaders across numerous capacities and lines of business can:

- Determine what they have to settle on the choice and when they'll think of it as complete
- Understand the choice with regards to related cycles, systems, and occasions
- Visualize data that would somehow be troublesome or difficult to comprehend through content and numbers alone
- Apply this way to deal with other choice situations.

It is the place choice empowering programming is going. Today, a topic master—a danger chief, for example—can display a business choice and execute it without pulling IT assets from different assignments. In this manner, operationalizing data-driven options was incomprehensible even a couple of years back—yet a reality today in associations, everything equal, in all enterprises.

CHAPTER THREE - BUILDING AND OPERATIONALIZING A DATA PROCESSING SYSTEM

Data pipeline design: Building away from ingestion to examination

Data pipelines transport crude data from programming as-an administration (SaaS) stages and data set sources to data stockrooms for use by analysis and business knowledge (BI) tools. Designers can construct pipelines themselves by composing code and physically interfacing with source databases — or they can abstain from rehashing an already solved problem and utilize a SaaS data pipeline.

To see the amount of unrest data, pipeline-as-an administration seems to be. How much work goes into amassing an outdated data pipeline? We should survey the significant parts and structure of data pipelines, just as the developments accessible for duplicating data.

Data pipeline design

A data pipeline design is the plan and structure of code and systems that duplicate, purify or change varying, and course source data to objective systems, for example, data distribution centers and data lakes.

Three components add to the speed with which data travels through a data pipeline:

- Rate, or throughput, is how much data a pipeline can measure inside a set measure of time.

- Data pipeline dependability requires singular systems inside a data pipeline to be issue lenient. A reliable data pipeline with worked in reviewing, logging, and approval systems guarantee data quality.

- Latency is the time required for a solitary unit of data to go through the pipeline. Inactivity relates more to reaction time than to volume or throughput. Low dormancy can be costly to keep up regarding both cost and handling assets, and an endeavor should find some kind of harmony to boost the worth it gets from the examination.

Data specialists should try to enhance these parts of the pipeline to suit the association's needs. An endeavor must think about business targets, cost, and computational assets' accessibility when planning its pipeline.

Planning a data pipeline

A data pipeline design is layered. Every subsystem takes care of the following until data arrives at its objective.

Data sources

As far as plumbing — we are discussing pipelines, all things considered — data sources are the wells, lakes, and streams where associations first accumulate data. SaaS sellers uphold many potential data sources, and each association has many others on their systems. As the top layer in a data pipeline, data sources are critical to its plan. Without quality data, there's nothing to ingest and travel through the pipeline.

Ingestion

The ingestion parts of a data pipeline are the cycles that read data from data sources — the siphons and water systems in our pipes similarity. An extraction cycle peruses from every data source utilizing application programming interfaces (API) gave by the data source. Before you can compose code that calls the APIs, however, you need to make sense of what data you need to disengage through a cycle called data profiling — inspecting data for its attributes and structure, and assessing how well it fits a business reason.

After the data is profiled, it's ingested, either as clusters or through streaming.

Cluster ingestion and streaming ingestion

Cluster handling is when sets of records are removed and worked on as a gathering. Cluster preparation is consecutive, and the ingestion instrument peruses cycles and yields gatherings of records as per measures set by engineers and investigators already. However, the process doesn't look for new records and continuously moves them along; instead, it runs on a timetable or acts dependent on outside triggers.

Streaming is an elective data ingestion worldview where data sources naturally go along singular records or units of data individually. All associations use group ingestion for various sorts of data. Simultaneously, undertakings utilize streaming ingestion just when they need close, continuous data for applications or analyses requiring conceivable base dormancy.

Contingent upon a venture's data change needs, the data is either moved into an organizing region or sent legitimately alongside its stream.

Change

When data is separated from source systems, its structure or organization may be balanced. Cycles that change data are the desalination stations, treatment plants, and individual water pipeline's water channels.

Changes incorporate coded planning esteems to more enlightening ones, separating, and accumulation. The blend is an especially significant sort of change. It integrates database joins, where connections encoded in social data models can bring related numerous tables, sections, and records.

Any changes' circumstance relies upon what data replication measure an endeavor chooses to use in its data pipeline: ETL (remove, change, burden) or ELT (separate, load, change). ETL, a more seasoned technology utilized with on-premises data distribution centers, can change data before it's stacked to its objective. ELT, used with present-day cloud-based data stockrooms, loads data without applying any changes. Data customers would then apply their changes to data inside a data stockroom or data lake.

Objections

Objections are the water pinnacles and holding tanks of the data pipeline. A data distribution center is a principal objective for data reproduced through the pipeline. These specific databases contain the entirety of an endeavor's cleaned, aced data in an incorporated area for use in examination, detailing, and business insight by experts and chiefs.

Less-organized data can stream into data lakes, where data experts and data researchers can get to the huge amounts of rich and minable data.

Finally, a venture may take care of data into an analysis tool or administration that legitimately acknowledges data takes care of.

Checking

Data pipelines are unpredictable systems that comprise programming, equipment, and systems administration segments, all dependent upon disappointments. To keep the pipeline operational and fit for extricating and stacking data, designers must compose observing, logging, and making code aware of help data engineers oversee execution and resolve any issues that emerge.

Data pipeline technologies and strategies

Regarding utilizing data pipelines, organizations have two options: compose their own or use a SaaS pipeline.

Associations can request that their designers compose, testing, and keeping up the code required for a data pipeline. All the while, they may utilize a few toolbox and structures:

- Workflow the executive's instruments can diminish the trouble of making a data pipeline. Open source tools like Airflow and Luigistructure the cycles that make up the pipeline, naturally resolve conditions and give designers an approach to imagine and compose data work processes.

- Event and informing structures like Apache Kafka and RabbitMQ permit organizations to create quicker, better data from their current applications. These structures catch business applications' occasions, making them accessible as high-throughput streams and empowering correspondence between various systems utilizing their conventions.

- Timely booking of cycles is additionally basic in any data pipeline. Numerous instruments permit clients to make definite timetables administering data ingestion, change, and stacking to objections, from the essential utility to whole committed remaining burden robotization stages.

It streams the entirety of your data legitimately to your examination stockroom.

Human-made consciousness and Data Engineering

A lot is on the line. Computer-based intelligence vows help businesses precisely anticipate changing business sector elements, improve the nature of contributions, increment effectiveness, advance client encounters, and decrease hierarchical danger by making business, cycles, and items more clever. Such serious advantages present a convincing allurement to receive AI shortly.

Computer-based intelligence is discovering its way into all ways of utilizations from AI-driven proposals, self-ruling vehicles, menial helpers, proactive analysis, and items that adjust to clients' necessities and inclinations. Yet, the same number of and differed as AI-empowered applications seem to be, they all offer a common goal at their center—to ingest data from numerous sources and determine significant bits of knowledge or insight from it.

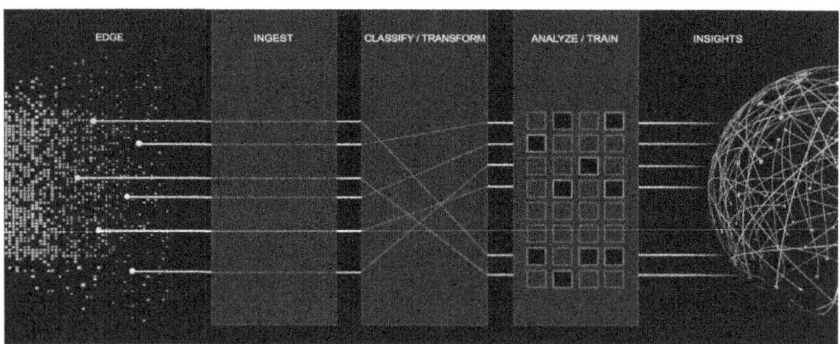

In any case, as much guarantee as AI holds to quicken development, increment business nimbleness, improve client encounters, and a large group of different advantages, a few organizations are receiving it quicker than others. For a few, there is vulnerability since AI appears to be excessively convoluted. For them, getting from here to there—or, all the more explicitly, from ingest to bits of knowledge—

may appear to be too overwhelming a test. That might be because no different business or IT activity guarantees more regarding results or is additionally requesting the infrastructure on which it is run.

Simulated intelligence done well looks basic from an external perspective. Escaped see behind each extraordinary AI-empowered application, in any case, lies a data pipeline that moves data—the major structure square of human-made reasoning—from ingest through a few phases of data arrangement, change, analysis, AI, and profound learning model preparing, and retraining through derivation to yield progressively exact choices or experiences.

The AI data pipeline is neither straight nor fixed, and even to educated onlookers, it can appear to be that creation grade AI is chaotic and troublesome. What's more, as associations move from experimentation and prototyping to sending AI underway, their first test is to implant AI into their current examination data pipeline and fabricate a data pipeline that can use existing data archives. Notwithstanding this goal, worries about incorporating intricacy may linger as perhaps the best test to select AI in their associations. However, it doesn't need to be like that.

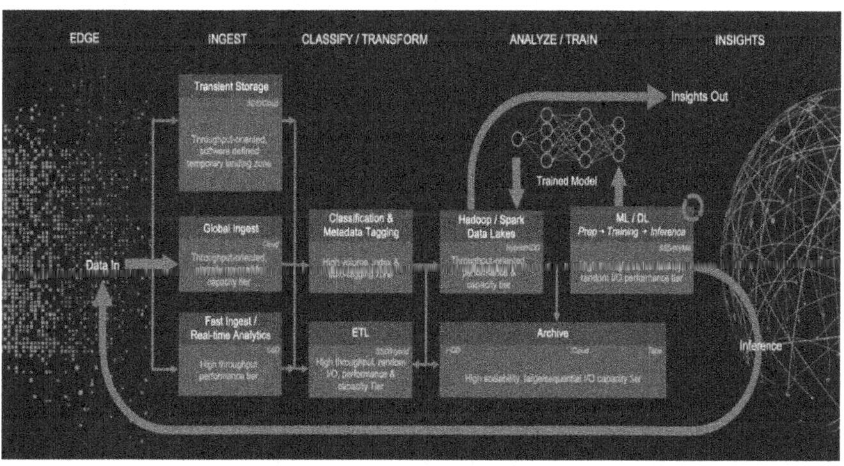

Various phases of the data pipeline display impressive I/O attributes and advantages from complimentary capacity infrastructure. For instance, ingest or data assortment profits by the adaptability of programming characterized capacity at the edge, and requests high throughput. Information arrangement and change stages include collecting, normalizing, characterizing data, and advancing it with useful metadata requiring very high throughput, with both little and enormous I/O. Model preparation requires an exhibition level that can uphold the exceptionally equal cycles associated with AI preparation and profound learning models with incredibly high throughput and low inactivity.

Retraining of models with induction doesn't need as much throughput yet requests incredibly low inactivity. Furthermore, the document requests an exceptionally versatile limit level for cold and dynamic file data that is throughput arranged and underpins enormous I/O, streaming, consecutive composes. Any of these may happen on-premises or in a private or public cloud, contingent upon necessities.

These changing necessities for versatility, execution, sending adaptability, and interoperability are a difficult task. In any case, data science efficiency is needy upon the general data pipeline's viability and not merely the exhibition of the infrastructure that has the ML/DL outstanding tasks at hand. It requires an arrangement of programming and framework advances to fulfill these prerequisites along the whole data pipeline.

Numerous merchants are hustling to answer the call for elite ML/DL infrastructure. IBM accomplishes more by offering an arrangement of adequate broadness to address the shifted needs at each phase of the AI data pipeline—from ingest to experiences. IBM answers the call with an exhaustive arrangement of programming characterized capacity items that empower clients to fabricate or improve their data pipelines with abilities and cost qualities that are ideal for each stage, bringing execution, nimbleness, and effectiveness to the whole data pipeline

Documentation

Operationalize a data analysis pipeline

Information pipelines underlie numerous data analysis arrangements. As the name recommends, a data pipeline takes in crude data, cleans, reshapes it varying, and afterward commonly performs computations or accumulations before putting away the prepared data. Customers, reports, or APIs expend the handled data. A data pipeline must give repeatable outcomes, regardless of whether on a timetable or when set off by new data.

This article depicts how to operationalize your data pipelines for repeatability, utilizing Oozie running on HDInsight Hadoop bunches. The model situation strolls you through a data pipeline that plans and cycles aircraft flight time-arrangement data.

The info data is a level record containing a cluster of flight data for one month in the accompanying situation. This flight data incorporates data, for example, the inception and objective air terminal, the miles flown, the takeoff and appearance times, etc. This pipeline aims to sum up day by day carrier execution, where every aircraft has one line for every day with the normal flight and appearance delays in minutes and the all-out miles have flown that day.

TABLE 1

YEAR	MONTH	DAY_OF_MONTH	CARRIER	AVG_DEP_DELAY	AVG_ARR_DELAY	TOTAL_DISTANCE
2017	1	3	AA	10.142229	7.862926	2644539
2017	1	3	AS	9.435449	5.482143	572289
2017	1	3	DL	6.935409	-2.1893024	1909696

The model pipeline holds up until another period's flight data shows up at that point stores that itemized flight data into your Apache Hive data distribution center for extended haul examinations. The pipeline additionally makes a lot of littler dataset that sums up only the day by day flight data. By day, flight rundown data is sent to a SQL Database to give reports, for example, for a site.

The accompanying chart delineates the model pipeline.

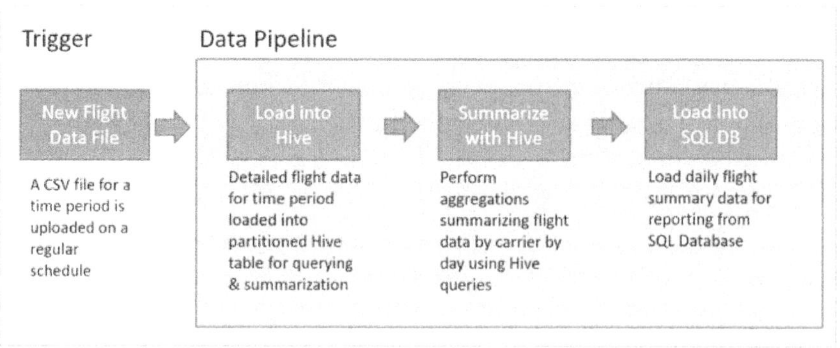
Trigger
Data Pipeline
New Flight Data File
A CSV file for a time period is uploaded on a regular schedule
Load into Hive
Detailed flight data for time period loaded into partitioned Hive table for querying & summarization
Summarize with Hive
Perform aggregations summarizing flight data by carrier by day using Hive queries
Load into SQL DB
Load daily flight summary data for reporting from SQL Database

Apache Oozie arrangement diagram

This pipeline utilizes Apache Oozie running on an HDInsight Hadoop bunch.

Oozie depicts its pipelines regarding activities, work processes, and facilitators. Activities decide the real work to perform, for example, running a Hive inquiry. Work processes characterize the grouping of activities. Organizers describe the timetable for when the work process is run. Organizers can likewise sit tight to access new data before dispatching an occasion of the work process.

The accompanying graph shows the significant level plan of this model Oozie pipeline.

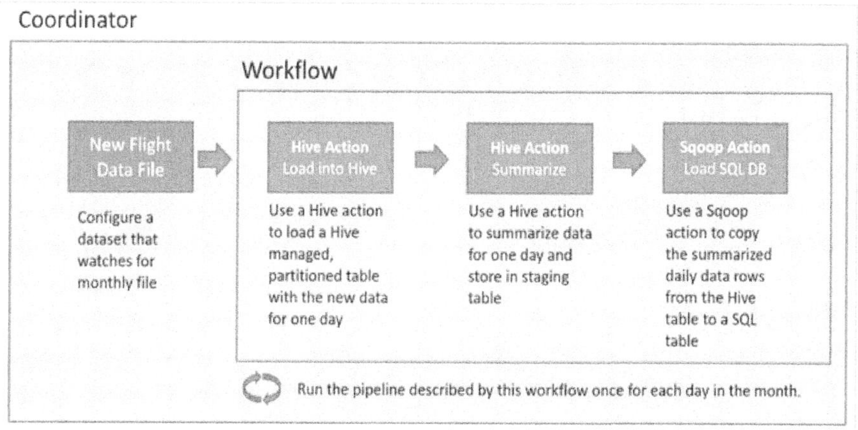

Arrangement Azure assets

This pipeline requires an Azure SQL Database and an HDInsight Hadoop bunch in a comparative region. The Azure SQL Database stores both the rundown data delivered by the pipeline and the Oozie Metadata Store.

Arrangement Azure SQL Database

1. Make an Azure SQL Database. See Create an Azure SQL Database in the Azure section.

2. To ensure that your HDInsight group can get to the associated Azure SQL Database, design Azure SQL Database firewall rules to permit Azure services and assets to get to the worker. You can empower this choice in the Azure entry by choosing Set worker firewall, and choosing ON underneath Allow Azure services and assets to get to this worker for Azure SQL Database. For more data, see Create and oversee IP firewall rules.

3. Use the Query manager to execute the accompanying SQL explanations to make them every day flights' table that will store the summed up data from each run of the pipeline.

SQLCopy

```
Make TABLE day by day flights
(
YEAR INT,
MONTH INT,
DAY_OF_MONTH INT,
Transporter CHAR(2),
AVG_DEP_DELAY FLOAT,
AVG_ARR_DELAY FLOAT,
TOTAL_DISTANCE FLOAT
)
GO
Make CLUSTERED INDEX dailyflights_clustered_index on
```

dailyflights(YEAR,MONTH,DAY_OF_MONTH,CARRIER)

GO

Your Azure SQL Database is presently prepared.

Arrangement an Apache Hadoop Cluster

Make an Apache Hadoop bunch with a custom megastore. During bunch creation from the entry, from the Storage tab, guarantee you select your SQL Database under Metastore settings; for more data on choosing a megastore, see Select a custom megastore during bunch creation. For more data on bunch creation, see Get Started with HDInsight on Linux.

Confirm SSH burrowing set up

To utilize the Oozie Web Console to see the status of your organizer and work process occasions, set up an SSH passage to your HDInsight group. For more data, see the SSH Tunnel.

Note

You can likewise utilize Chrome with the Foxy Proxy expansion to peruse your group's web assets over the SSH burrow. Arrange it to intermediary all demand through the host localhost on the passage's port 9876. This methodology is viable with the Windows Subsystem for Linux, otherwise called Bash on Windows 10.

1. Run the accompanying order to open an SSH passage to your group, where CLUSTERNAME is the name of your bunch:

cmd duplicate

ssh - C2qTnNf - D 9876 sshuser@CLUSTERNAME-ssh.azurehdinsight.net

2. Verify the passage is operational by exploring to Ambari on your head hub by perusing to:

http://headnodehost:8080

3. To access the Oozie Web Console from inside Ambari, explore to Oozie > Quick Links > [Active server] > Oozie Web UI.

Arrange Hive

Transfer data

1. Download a model CSV document that contains flight data for one month. Download its ZIP record 2017-01-FlightData.zip from the HDInsight GitHub archive and unfasten it to the CSV document 2017-01-FlightData.csv.

2. Copy this CSV document up to the Azure Storage account appended to your HDInsight bunch and spot it in the/model/data/flight envelope.

a. Use SCP to duplicate your nearby machine's records to the neighborhood storage of your HDInsight group head hub.

cmdCopy

scp ./2017-01-FlightData.csv sshuser@CLUSTERNAME-ssh.azurehdinsight.net:2017-01-FlightData.csv

b. Use the ssh order to associate with your group. Alter the order underneath by supplanting CLUSTERNAME with the name of your group, and afterward enter the order:

cmdCopy

ssh sshuser@CLUSTERNAME-ssh.azurehdinsight.net

c. From your ssh meeting, utilize the HDFS to duplicate the record from your head hub nearby capacity to Azure Storage.

BashCopy

hadoop fs - mkdir/model/data/flights

hdfs dfs - put ./2017-01-FlightData.csv/model/data/flights/2017-01-FlightData.csv

Make tables

The example data is presently accessible. In any case, the pipeline requires two Hive tables for preparing, one for the approaching data (crude flights), and one for the summed up data (flights). Make these tables in Ambari as follows.

1. Log in to Ambari by exploring to http://headnodehost:8080.
2. From the rundown of services, select Hive.

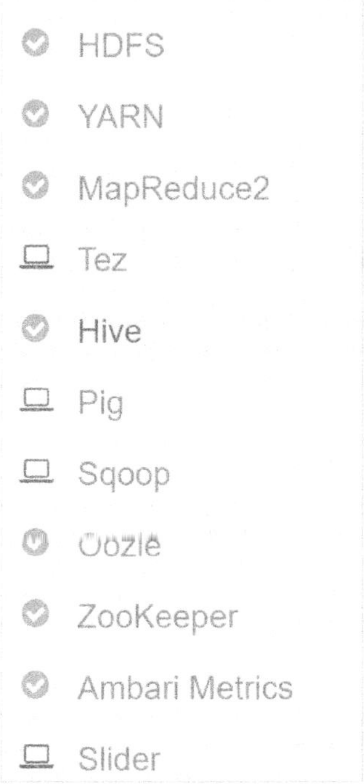

HDFS
YARN
MapReduce2
Tez
Hive
Pig
Sqoop
Oozie
ZooKeeper
Ambari Metrics
Slider

1. Select **Go To View** next to the Hive View 2.0 label.

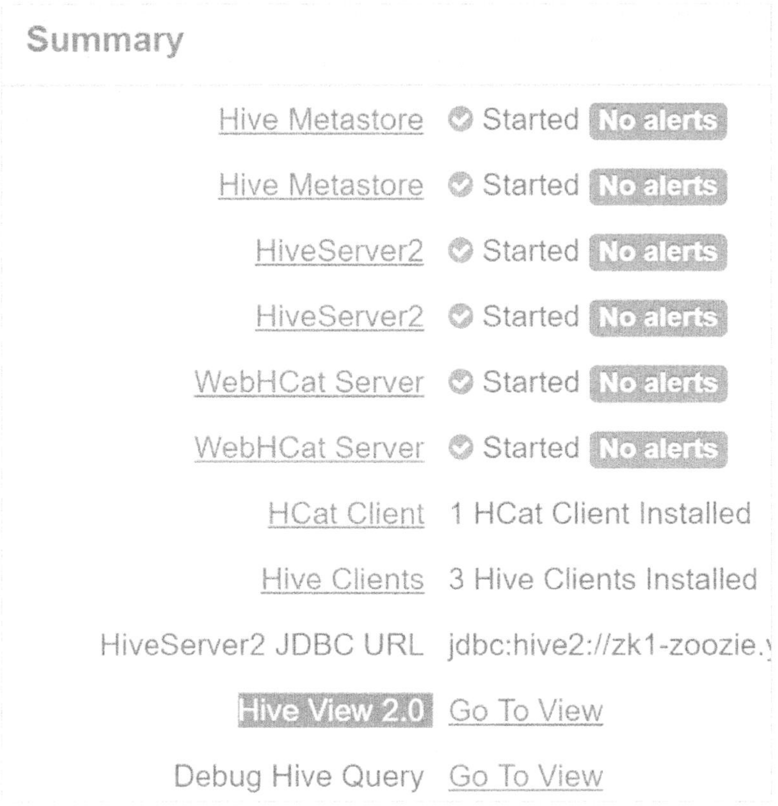

2. In the query text area, paste the following statements to create the raw flight table. The rawFlightstable provides a schema-on-read for the CSV files within the /example/data/flights folder in Azure Storage.

SQLCopy

```
CREATE EXTERNAL TABLE IF NOT EXISTS raw flights (

   CARRIER STRING,
YEAR INT,
MONTH INT,
   DAY_OF_MONTH INT,
```

FL_DATE STRING,
FL_NUM STRING,
ORIGIN STRING,
DEST STRING,
DISTANCE FLOAT)
ARR_DELAY FLOAT,
DEP_DELAY FLOAT,
ACTUAL_ELAPSED_TIME FLOAT,

ROW FORMAT SERDE 'org.apache.hadoop.hive.serde2.OpenCSVSerde'
WITH SERDEPROPERTIES
(
“separatorChar” = “,”,
“quoteChar” = “\”“
)
LOCATION '/example/ flights/' data

3. Select **Execute** to create the table.

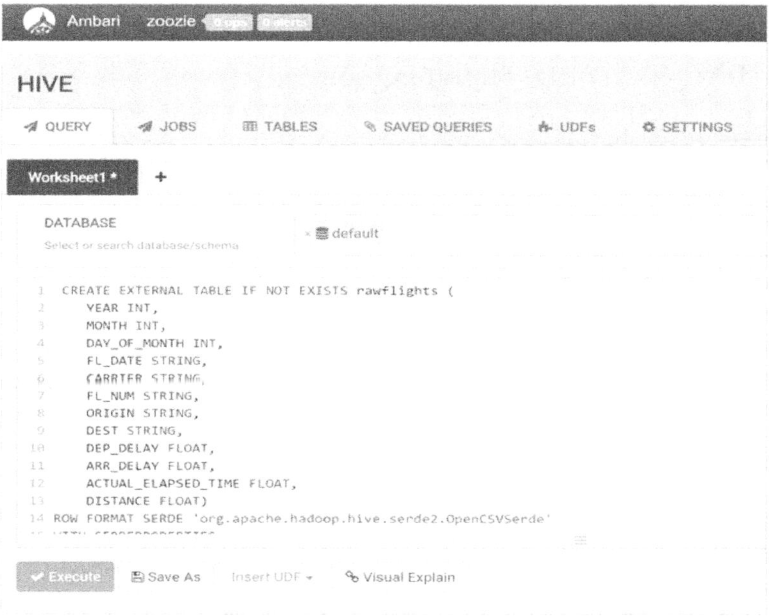

Ambari zoozie 0 ops 0 alerts

HIVE

QUERY JOBS TABLES SAVED QUERIES UDFs SETTINGS

Worksheet1 * +

DATABASE
Select or search database/schema
default

```
CREATE EXTERNAL TABLE IF NOT EXISTS rawflights (
    YEAR INT,
    MONTH INT,
    DAY_OF_MONTH INT,
    FL_DATE STRING,
    CARRIER STRING,
    FL_NUM STRING,
    ORIGIN STRING,
    DEST STRING,
    DEP_DELAY FLOAT,
    ARR_DELAY FLOAT,
    ACTUAL_ELAPSED_TIME FLOAT,
    DISTANCE FLOAT)
ROW FORMAT SERDE 'org.apache.hadoop.hive.serde2.OpenCSVSerde'
```

Execute Save As Insert UDF Visual Explain

4. To create the flight table, replace the text in the query text area with the following statements. The flights' table is a Hive-managed table that partitions data loaded into it by year, month, and day of the month. This table will contain all verifiable flight data, with the most minimal granularity present in one column's source data for every flight.

5. SQLCopy

```
SET hive.exec.dynamic.partition.mode=nonstrict;

CREATE TABLE flights
(
   ORIGIN STRING,
FL_DATE STRING,
   CARRIER STRING,

FL_NUM STRING,
ARR_DELAY FLOAT,
   DEP_DELAY FLOAT,
   DEST STRING,
   ACTUAL_ELAPSED_TIME FLOAT,
      DISTANCE FLOAT

)
PARTITIONED BY (YEAR INT, MONTH INT,
DAY_OF_MONTH INT)
ROW FORMAT SERDE
'org.apache.hadoop.hive.serde2.OpenCSVSerde'
WITH SERDEPROPERTIES
(
   "separatorChar" = ",",
   "quoteChar"    = "\""
);
```

6. Select **Execute** to create the table.

Make the Oozie work process

Pipelines commonly measure data in bunches by a given time stretch. For this situation, the pipeline measures the flight data day by day. This methodology considers the data CSV documents to show up day by day, week after week, month to month, or yearly.

The example work process measures the flight data step by step in three significant advances:

1. Run a Hive question to separate the data for that day's date extend from the source CSV record spoke to by the rawFlightstable and the data into the flights' table.

2. Run a Hive inquiry to powerfully make an organizing table in Hive for the afternoon, which contains a duplicate of the flight data summed up by day and transporter.

3. Use Apache Sqoop to duplicate all the data from the daily arranging table in Hive to the objective day by day flights table in Azure SQL Database. Sqoop peruses the source lines from the data behind the Hive table dwelling in Azure Storage and burdens them into SQL Database utilizing a JDBC association.

An Oozie work process arranges these three stages.

1. From your neighborhood workstation, make a record called job.properties. Utilize the content underneath as the beginning substance for the record. At that point update the qualities for your particular condition. The table underneath the content sums up every one of the properties and demonstrates where you can discover the qualities for your own condition.textCopy

```
nameNode=wasbs://[CONTAINERNAME]@[ACCOUNTNAME
].blob.core.windows.net
jobTracker=[ACTIVERESOURCEMANAGER]:8050
queueName=default
oozie.use.system.libpath=true
appBase=wasbs://[CONTAINERNAME]@[ACCOUNTNAME].bl
ob.core.windows.net/oozie
oozie.wf.application.path=${appBase}/load_flights_by_day
hiveScriptLoadPartition=wasbs://[CONTAINERNAME]@[ACCO
UNTNAME].blob.core.windows.net/oozie/load_flights_by_day/hiv
e-load-flights-partition.hql
hiveScriptCreateDailyTable=wasbs://[CONTAINERNAME]@[AC
COUNTNAME].blob.core.windows.net/oozie/load_flights_by_day
/hive-create-daily-summary-table.hql
hiveDailyTableName=dailyflights${year}${month}${day}
hiveDataFolder=wasbs://[CONTAINERNAME]@[ACCOUNTN
AME].blob.core.windows.net/example/data/flights/day/${year}/${
month}/${day}
sqlDatabaseConnectionString="jdbc:sqlserver://[SERVERNAME].
database.windows.net;user=[USERNAME];password=[PASSWORD
];database=[DATABASENAME]"
sqlDatabaseTableName=dailyflights
year=2017
month=01
day=03
```

TABLE 2

Property	**Value source**
name node	The full path to the Azure Storage Container attached to your HDInsight cluster.
job tracker	The internal hostname to your active cluster's YARN head node. On the Ambari home page, select YARN from the list of services, then choose Active Resource Manager. The hostname URI is displayed at the top of the page. Append the port 8050.
queueName	The name of the YARN queue used when scheduling the Hive actions. Leave as default.
oozie.use.system.libpath	Leave as true.
appBase	The path to the subfolder in Azure Storage where you deploy the Oozie workflow and supporting files.
oozie.wf.application.path	The location of the Oozie workflow .xmlto run.

hiveScriptLoadPartition	The path in Azure Storage to the Hive query file hive-load-flights-partition.hql.
hiveScriptCreateDailyTable	The path in Azure Storage to the Hive query file hive-create-daily-summary-table.hql.
hiveDailyTableName	The dynamically generated name to use for the staging table.
hiveDataFolder	The path in Azure Storage to the data contained by the staging table.
sqlDatabaseConnectionString	The JDBC syntax connection string to your Azure SQL Database.
sqlDatabaseTableName	The name of the table in Azure SQL Database into which summary rows are inserted. Leave as daily flights.
year	The year component of the day for which flight summaries are computed. Leave as is.

month	The month component of the day for which flight summaries are computed. Leave as is.
day	The day of month component of the day for which flight summaries are computed. Leave as is.

1. From your nearby workstation, make a document called hive-load-flights-partition.hql. Utilize the code beneath as the substance for the record.SQLCopy

```
SET hive.exec.dynamic.partition.mode=nonstrict;

INSERT OVERWRITE TABLE flights
PARTITION (YEAR, MONTH, DAY_OF_MONTH)
SELECT
    CARRIER,
 FL_DATE,
    ORIGIN,
 DEST,
 FL_NUM,
    ACTUAL_ELAPSED_TIME,
    ARR_DELAY,
    DEP_DELAY,
    YEAR,
    MONTH
 DAY_OF_MONTH
    , DISTANCE,
```

FROM raw flights

WHERE year = ${year} AND month = ${month} AND day_of_month = ${day};

Oozie factors utilize the sentence structure ${variableName}. These factors are set in the job properties record. Oozie substitutes the genuine qualities at runtime.

1. From your neighborhood workstation, make a record called hive-make day by day synopsis table.hql. Utilize the code beneath as the substance for the record.SQLCopy

```
DROP TABLE ${hiveTableName};
CREATE EXTERNAL TABLE ${hiveTableName}
(
   YEAR INT,
   MONTH INT,
   DAY_OF_MONTH INT,
   AVG_ARR_DELAY FLOAT,
   AVG_DEP_DELAY FLOAT,
   CARRIER STRING,
TOTAL_DISTANCE FLOAT
)
```

Line FORMAT DELIMITED

FIELDS TERMINATED BY '\t' STORED AS TEXTFILE LOCATION '${hiveDataFolder}';

Addition OVERWRITE TABLE ${hiveTableName}

SELECT year, month, day_of_month, transporter, avg(dep_delay) avg_dep_delay, avg(arr_delay) avg_arr_delay, sum(distance) total_distance

FROM flights

Gathering BY year, month, day_of_month, transporter

HAVING year = ${year} AND month = ${month} AND day_of_month = ${day};

This inquiry makes an arranging table that will store just the summed up data for one day and observe the SELECT articulation that registers the normal postponements and complete separation flown by the transporter by day. The data embedded into this table put away at a known area (the way showed by the hiveDataFolder variable). It tends to be utilized as the hotspot for Sqoop in the following stage.

1. From your nearby workstation, make a document called workflow.xml. Utilize the code beneath as the substance for the document. These means above are communicated as isolated activities in the Oozie work process document.

XMLCopy

```
<workflow-app name="loadflightstable"
xmlns="uri:oozie:workflow:0.5">
    <start to = "RunHiveLoadFlightsScript"/>
    <action name="RunHiveLoadFlightsScript">
        <hive xmlns="uri:oozie:hive-action:0.2">
            <job-tracker>${jobTracker}</job-tracker>
            <name-node>${nameNode}</name-node>
            <configuration>
            <property>
                <name>mapred.job.queue.name</name>
```

```
            <value>${queueName}</value>
        </property>
        </configuration>
        <script>${hiveScriptLoadPartition}</script>
        <param>year=${year}</param>
        <param>month=${month}</param>
        <param>day=${day}</param>
    </hive>
    <ok to="RunHiveCreateDailyFlightTableScript"/>
    <error to="fail"/>
</action>

<action name="RunHiveCreateDailyFlightTableScript">
    <hive xmlns="uri:oozie:hive-action:0.2">
        <job-tracker>${jobTracker}</job-tracker>
        <name-node>${nameNode}</name-node>
        <configuration>
        <property>
            <name>mapred.job.queue.name</name>
            <value>${queueName}</value>
        </property>
        </configuration>
        <script>${hiveScriptCreateDailyTable}</script>
        <param>hiveTableName=${hiveDailyTableName}</para
        m>
        <param>year=${year}</param>
        <param>month=${month}</param>
        <param>day=${day}</param>
        <param>hiveDataFolder=${hiveDataFolder}/${year}/${
        month}/${day}</param>
    </hive>
    <ok to="RunSqoopExport"/>
    <error to="fail"/>
</action>
```

```
    <action name="RunSqoopExport">
      <sqoop xmlns="uri:oozie:sqoop-action:0.2">
        <job-tracker>${jobTracker}</job-tracker>
        <name-node>${nameNode}</name-node>
        <configuration>
        <property>
          <name>mapred.compress.map.output</name>
          <value>true</value>
        </property>
        </configuration>
        <arg>export</arg>
        <arg>--connect</arg>
        <arg>${sqlDatabaseConnectionString}</arg>
        <arg>--table</arg>
        <arg>${sqlDatabaseTableName}</arg>
        <arg>--export-dir</arg>
        <arg>${hiveDataFolder}/${year}/${month}/${day}</ar
        g>
        <arg>-m</arg>
        <arg>1</arg>
        <arg>--input-fields-terminated-by</arg>
        <arg>"\t"</arg>
        <archive>mssql-jdbc-7.0.0.jre8.jar</archive>
        </sqoop>
      <ok to="end"/>
      <error to="fail"/>
    </action>
    <kill name="fail">
      <message>Job failed, error
      message[${wf:errorMessage(wf:lastErrorNode())}]
      </message>
    </kill>
    <end name="end"/>
  </workflow-app>
```

The two Hive inquiries are gotten to by their way in Azure Storage, and the staying variable qualities are given by the job. properties record. This document arranges the work process to run for the date January 3, 2017.

Convey and run the Oozie work process

Use SCP from your slam meeting to convey your Oozie work process (workflow.xml), the Hive questions (hive-load-flights-partition.hql, and hive-make day by day synopsis table.hql), and the activity arrangement (job.properties). In Oozie, just the job.properties record can exist on the nearby storage of the head node. All different records must be put away in HDFS for this situation Azure Storage. The Sqoop activity utilized by the work process relies upon a JDBC driver for speaking with your SQL Database, which must be replicated from the head hub to HDFS.

1. Create the load_flights_by_daysubfolder underneath the client's way in the nearby storage of the head hub. From your open ssh meeting, execute the accompanying order:

BashCopy

mkdir load_flights_by_day

2. Copy all documents in the current index (the workflow.xml and job.propertiesfiles) up to the load_flights_by_daysubfolder. From your neighborhood workstation, execute the accompanying order:

cmdCopy

scp ./* sshuser@CLUSTERNAME-ssh.azurehdinsight.net:load_flights_by_day

3. Copy work process records to HDFS. From your open ssh meeting, execute the accompanying orders:

BashCopy

cd load_flights_by_day

hadoop fs - mkdir - p/oozie/load_flights_by_day

hdfs dfs - put ./*/oozie/load_flights_by_day

4. Copy mssql-jdbc-7.0.0.jre8.jarfrom the neighborhood head hub to the work process organizer in HDFS. Change order varying if your group contains an alternate container record. Update workflow.xml varying to mirror an alternate container document. From your open ssh meeting, execute the accompanying order:

BashCopy

hdfs dfs - put/usr/share/java/sqljdbc_7.0/enu/mssql-jdbc*.jar/oozie/load_flights_by_day

5. Run the work process. From your open ssh meeting, execute the accompanying order:

BashCopy

oozie work - config job.properties - run

7. Observe the status utilizing the Oozie Web Console. From inside Ambari, select Oozie, Quick Links, and afterward Oozie Web Console, select all Jobs under the Jobs tab.

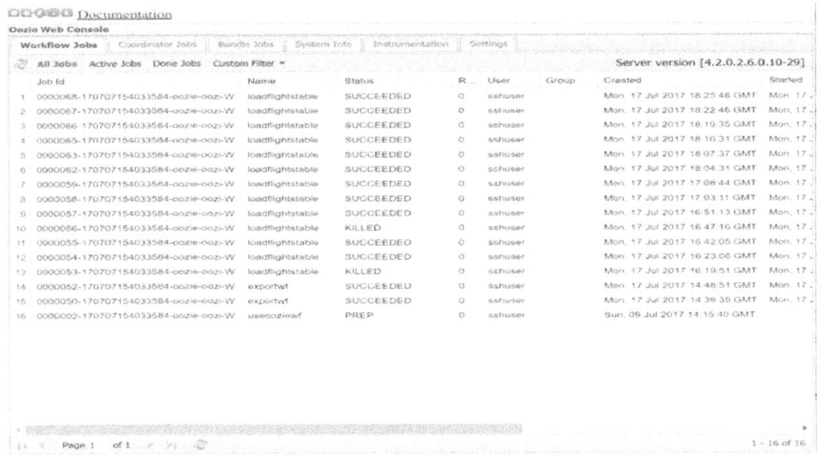

	Job Id	Name	Status	R...	User	Group	Created	Started
1	0000068-170707154033584-oozie-oozi-W	loadflightstable	SUCCEEDED	0	sshuser		Mon, 17 Jul 2017 18:25:48 GMT	Mon, 17 ...
2	0000067-170707154033584-oozie-oozi-W	loadflightstable	SUCCEEDED	0	sshuser		Mon, 17 Jul 2017 18:22:46 GMT	Mon, 17 ...
3	0000066-170707154033584-oozie-oozi-W	loadflightstable	SUCCEEDED	0	sshuser		Mon, 17 Jul 2017 18:19:35 GMT	Mon, 17 ...
4	0000065-170707154033584-oozie-oozi-W	loadflightstable	SUCCEEDED	0	sshuser		Mon, 17 Jul 2017 18:16:31 GMT	Mon, 17 ...
5	0000063-170707154033584-oozie-oozi-W	loadflightstable	SUCCEEDED	0	sshuser		Mon, 17 Jul 2017 18:07:37 GMT	Mon, 17 ...
6	0000062-170707154033584-oozie-oozi-W	loadflightstable	SUCCEEDED	0	sshuser		Mon, 17 Jul 2017 18:04:31 GMT	Mon, 17 ...
7	0000059-170707154033584-oozie-oozi-W	loadflightstable	SUCCEEDED	0	sshuser		Mon, 17 Jul 2017 17:08:44 GMT	Mon, 17 ...
8	0000058-170707154033584-oozie-oozi-W	loadflightstable	SUCCEEDED	0	sshuser		Mon, 17 Jul 2017 17:03:11 GMT	Mon, 17 ...
9	0000057-170707154033584-oozie-oozi-W	loadflightstable	SUCCEEDED	0	sshuser		Mon, 17 Jul 2017 16:51:13 GMT	Mon, 17 ...
10	0000056-170707154033584-oozie-oozi-W	loadflightstable	KILLED	0	sshuser		Mon, 17 Jul 2017 16:47:16 GMT	Mon, 17 ...
11	0000055-170707154033584-oozie-oozi-W	loadflightstable	SUCCEEDED	0	sshuser		Mon, 17 Jul 2017 16:42:05 GMT	Mon, 17 ...
12	0000054-170707154033584-oozie-oozi-W	loadflightstable	SUCCEEDED	0	sshuser		Mon, 17 Jul 2017 16:23:06 GMT	Mon, 17 ...
13	0000053-170707154033584-oozie-oozi-W	loadflightstable	KILLED	0	sshuser		Mon, 17 Jul 2017 16:19:51 GMT	Mon, 17 ...
14	0000052-170707154033584-oozie-oozi-W	exportwf	SUCCEEDED	0	sshuser		Mon, 17 Jul 2017 14:48:51 GMT	Mon, 17 ...
15	0000050-170707154033584-oozie-oozi-W	exportwf	SUCCEEDED	0	sshuser		Mon, 17 Jul 2017 14:39:39 GMT	Mon, 17 ...
16	0000002-170707154033584-oozie-oozi-W	useooziewf	PREP	0	sshuser		Sun, 09 Jul 2017 14:15:40 GMT	

1. When the status is SUCCEEDED, question the SQL Database table to see the embedded columns. Utilizing the Azure gateway, explore the sheet for your SQL Database, select Tools, and open the Query Editor.

SQLCopy

SELECT * FROM every day flights

Since the work process runs for the single test day, you can wrap this work process with an organizer that plans the work process to run day by day.

Run the work process with a facilitator

To plan this work process with the goal that it runs day by day (or throughout the days in a date extend), you can utilize a facilitator. An organizer is characterized by a XML document, for instance coordinator.xml:XMLCopy

<coordinator-app name="daily_export" start="2017-01-01T00:00Z" end="2017-01-05T00:00Z" frequency="${coord:days(1)}" timezone="UTC" xmlns="uri:oozie:coordinator:0.4">

<datasets>

```
    <dataset name="ds_input1" frequency="${coord:days(1)}"
    initial-instance="2016-12-31T00:00Z" timezone="UTC">
        <uri-template>${sourceDataFolder}${YEAR}-
        ${MONTH}-FlightData.csv</uri-template>
        <done-flag></done-flag>
    </dataset>
</datasets>
<input-events>
    <data-in name="event_input1" dataset="ds_input1">
        <instance>${coord:current(0)}</instance>
    </data-in>
</input-events>
<action>
    <workflow>
        <app-path>${appBase}/load_flights_by_day</app-path>
        <configuration>
            <property>
                <name>year</name>
                <value>${coord:formatTime(coord:nominalTime(),
                'yyyy')}</value>
            </property>
            <property>
                <name>month</name>
                <value>${coord:formatTime(coord:nominalTime(),
                'MM')}</value>
            </property>
            <property>
                <name>day</name>
                <value>${coord:formatTime(coord:nominalTime(),
                'dd')}</value>
            </property>
            <property>
                <name>hiveScriptLoadPartition</name>
                <value>${hiveScriptLoadPartition}</value>
```

```
</property>
<property>
   <name>hiveScriptCreateDailyTable</name>
   <value>${hiveScriptCreateDailyTable}</value>
</property>
<property>
   <name>hiveDailyTableNamePrefix</name>
   <value>${hiveDailyTableNamePrefix}</value>
</property>
<property>
   <name>hiveDailyTableName</name>
<value>${hiveDailyTableNamePrefix}${coord:formatTi
me(coord:nominalTime(),
'yyyy')}${coord:formatTime(coord:nominalTime(),
'MM')}${coord:formatTime(coord:nominalTime(),
'dd')}</value>
</property>
<property>
   <name>hiveDataFolderPrefix</name>
   <value>${hiveDataFolderPrefix}</value>
</property>
<property>
   <name>hiveDataFolder</name>
<value>${hiveDataFolderPrefix}${coord:formatTime(c
oord:nominalTime(),
'yyyy')}/${coord:formatTime(coord:nominalTime(),
'MM')}/${coord:formatTime(coord:nominalTime(),
'dd')}</value>
</property>
<property>
   <name>sqlDatabaseConnectionString</name>
   <value>${sqlDatabaseConnectionString}</value>
</property>
<property>
```

```
            <name>sqlDatabaseTableName</name>
            <value>${sqlDatabaseTableName}</value>
          </property>
        </configuration>
      </workflow>
    </action>
</coordinator-app>
```

As should be obvious, most of the organizer is simply passing arrangement data to the work process case. In any case, there are a couple of significant things to call out.

- Point 1: The beginning and end ascribe on the facilitator application component itself control the period over which the organizer runs.

Copy

```
<coordinator-app ... start="2017-01-01T00:00Z" end="2017-01-05T00:00Z" frequency="${coord:days(1)}" ...>
```

A facilitator is liable for booking activities inside the beginning and end date extends, as indicated by the span determined by the recurrence property. Each planned activity, therefore, runs the work process as designed. In the organizer definition, the facilitator is designed to run activities from January 1, 2017, to January 5, 2017. The recurrence is set to one day by the Oozie Expression Language recurrence articulation ${coord: days(1)}; these outcomes in the organizer planning an activity (and thus the work process) once every day. As in this model, the activity will be booked to run immediately for the date goes that is previously. The beginning of the date from which activity is booked to run is known as the ostensible time. For instance, to handle the data for January 1, 2017, the organizer will plan an activity with an ostensible season of 2017-01-01T00:00:00 GMT.

- Point 2: Within the date scope of the work process, the dataset component indicates were to glance in HDFS for the data for a specific date run, and arranges how Oozie decides if the data is accessible yet for handling.

XMLCopy

```
<dataset name="ds_input1" frequency="${coord:days(1)}" initial-instance="2016-12-31T00:00Z" timezone="UTC">
   <uri-template>${sourceDataFolder}${YEAR}-${MONTH}-
   FlightData.csv</uri-template>
   <done-flag></done-flag>
</dataset>
```

The way to the data in HDFS is manufactured progressively, as indicated by the articulation gave in the Uri-layout component. In this organizer, a recurrence of one day is additionally utilized with the dataset. While the beginning and end dates on the organizer component control when the activities are planned (and characterizes their ostensible occasions), the underlying instance and recurrence on the dataset control the computing of the data utilized in building the Uri-layout. For this situation, set the underlying event to one day before the organizer's beginning to guarantee that it gets the principal day's (1/1/2017) worth of data. The dataset's date computing moves forward from the estimation of the beginning instance(12/31/2016) progressing in additions of dataset recurrence (at some point) until it finds the latest date that doesn't relax set by the organizer (2017-01-01T00:00:00 GMT for the main activity).

The void done-hail component demonstrates that when Oozie checks for the presence of data at the named time, Oozie decides data whether accessible by the presence of a registry or document. For this situation, it's the presence of a CSV document. If a CSV record is available, Oozie expects the data is prepared and dispatches a work process occasion to handle the document. If there's no CSV document present, Oozie expects the data isn't yet prepared, and that run of the work process goes into a holding upstate.

- Point 3: The data in component indicates the specific timestamp to use as the ostensible time when supplanting the qualities in Uri-format for the related dataset.

XMLCopy

```
<data-in name="event_input1" dataset="ds_input1">
  <instance>${coord:current(0)}</instance>
</data-in>
```

For this situation, set the occasion to the articulation ${coord:current(0)}, which means utilizing the activity's ostensible season as initially planned by the organizer. At the end of the day, when the organizer plans the activity to run with an ostensible season of 01/01/2017, 01/01/2017 is what is utilized to supplant the YEAR (2017) and MONTH (01) factors in the URI layout. When the URI format is registered for this case, Oozie checks whether the normal registry or record is accessible and plans the next run of the work process appropriately.

The three going before guides join toward yielding a circumstance where the organizer plans preparing of the source data in a step by step style.

- Point 1: The facilitator begins with an ostensible date of 2017-01-01.
- Point 2: Oozie searches for data accessible in sourceDataFolder/2017-01-FlightData.csv.
- Point 3: When Oozie finds that record, it plans a case of the work process that will cycle the data for 2017-01-01. Oozie,

at that point, keeps preparing for 2017-01-02. This assessment rehashes up to, however, excluding 2017-01-05.

Similarly as with work processes, the setup of an organizer is characterized in a job.propertiesfile, which has a superset of the settings utilized by the work process.

textCopy

```
nameNode=wasbs://[CONTAINERNAME]@[ACCOUNTNAME
].blob.core.windows.net
jobTracker=[ACTIVERESOURCEMANAGER]:8050
queueName=default
oozie.use.system.libpath=true
appBase=wasbs://[CONTAINERNAME]@[ACCOUNTNAME].bl
ob.core.windows.net/oozie
oozie.coord.application.path=${appBase}
sourceDataFolder=wasbs://[CONTAINERNAME]@[ACCOUNT
NAME].blob.core.windows.net/example/data/flights/
hiveScriptLoadPartition=wasbs://[CONTAINERNAME]@[ACCO
UNTNAME].blob.core.windows.net/oozie/load_flights_by_day/hiv
e-load-flights-partition.hql
hiveScriptCreateDailyTable=wasbs://[CONTAINERNAME]@[AC
COUNTNAME].blob.core.windows.net/oozie/load_flights_by_day
/hive-create-daily-summary-table.hql
hiveDailyTableNamePrefix=dailyflights
hiveDataFolderPrefix=wasbs://[CONTAINERNAME]@[ACCOU
NTNAME].blob.core.windows.net/example/data/flights/day/
sqlDatabaseConnectionString="jdbc:sqlserver://[SERVERNAME].
database.windows.net;user=[USERNAME];password=[PASSWORD
];database=[DATABASENAME]"
sqlDatabaseTableName=dailyflights
```

The only new properties introduced in this job.properties file are:

TABLE 3

Property	Value source
oozie.coord.application.path	Indicates the location of the coordinator.xmlfile containing the Oozie coordinator to run.
hiveDailyTableNamePrefix	The prefix used when dynamically creating the table name of the staging table.
hiveDataFolderPrefix	The prefix of the path where all the staging tables will be stored.

Send and run the Oozie Coordinator

To run the pipeline with an organizer, continue likewise concerning the work process, aside from your work from an envelope one level over the envelope that contains your work process. This organizer show isolates the facilitators from the work processes on a circle to connect one organizer with various youngster work processes.

1. Use SCP from your nearby machine to duplicate the facilitator documents up to your group's head hub's neighborhood storage.

BashCopy

scp ./* sshuser@CLUSTERNAME-ssh.azurehdinsight.net:~

2. SSH into your head hub.

BashCopy

ssh sshuser@CLUSTERNAME-ssh.azurehdinsight.net

3. Copy the facilitator documents to HDFS.

BashCopy

hdfs dfs - put ./*/oozie/

4. Run the facilitator.

BashCopy

oozie work - config job.properties - run

5. Verify the status utilizing the Oozie Web Console, this time choosing the Coordinator Jobs tab, and afterward All positions.

1. Select an organizer occurrence to show the rundown of planned activities. For this situation, you should see four activities with ostensible occasions ranging from 1/1/2017 to 1/4/2017.

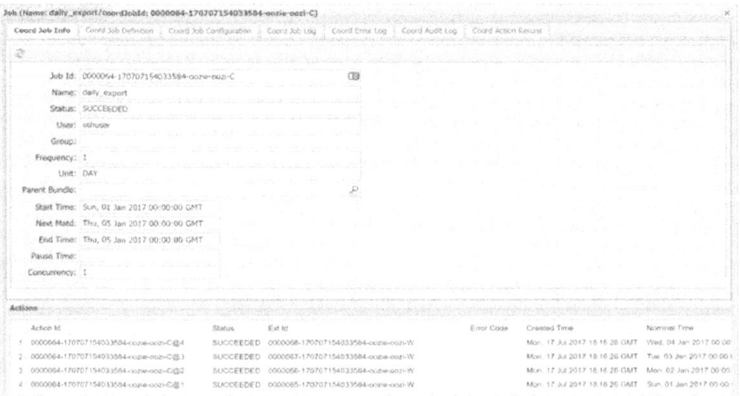

Each activity in this rundown compares to an occurrence of the work process that measures one day of data, where the beginning of that day is shown by the ostensible time.

CHAPTER FOUR - ENSURING QUALITY SOLUTION

Before data science becomes conventional, the emphasis on data quality was, for the most part, mentioned for the reports conveyed to internal or external clients. In recent times, because machine learning entails a huge quota of training data, the internal datasets within an organization are in excessive demand. Besides, the analytics are always hungry for data and persistently search for data assets that can practically increase value, resulting in a quick acquisition of new datasets or data sources not traversed or engaged before. This Vogue has coerced data management and acceptable practices of ensuring good data quality more principal than ever.

This chapter aims to provide a sustainable insight into creating a data channel that builds and maintains good data quality from the start. To put it simply, data quality is not something that can be structurally enhanced by spotting issues and resolving them. Alternatively, every organization should begin by producing data with good quality in the first place.

Firstly, we need to know what Data Quality is.

We can say that data quality is high when it meets its clients' expectations, decision-makers, downstream applications, and processes. A good example is of an item delivered by a producer. Excellent item quality isn't the business result, yet fills consumer loyalty and impacts the worth and life pattern of the object itself. Correspondingly, the data quality is a dominant attribute that could drive the value of the data and, consequently, impact aspects of the business outcome, such as regulatory adherence, customer satisfaction, or accuracy of decision making. There are five main criteria used to estimate data quality: Accuracy, Validity, Completeness, Timeliness, and Consistency.

Accuracy: Prescribed data needs to be accurate

Validity: Conforming to the standard set for it

Completeness: Data should have complete values and records

Timeliness: Data should be up to date

Consistency: The data should align well with preconceived patterns

For a few, the contrast between excellent data and "terrible" data appears to be straightforward. It's either right or off-base, exact or wrong. At the point when you go somewhat more profound, however, go a little deeper though, you'll discover the quality of your data rests on much more than just accuracy solely. If you've only got half the appropriate data, you can't have the high-quality data required, no matter how pristine. Likewise, technically accurate data but isn't timely can also impact its usefulness and comprehensive integrity. The standard for premium data quality can differ depending on the prerequisite and the nature of the data itself. For instance, a company's primary customer dataset needs to meet very high standards for the above-highlighted rules. Simultaneously, there could be a higher resistance of mistakes or deficiency for an outsider data source. For an association to convey data with excellent quality, it needs to oversee and control every data storage made in the pipeline from the earliest starting point as far as possible. Most organizations simply focus on the final data and invest in data quality control effort just before it is delivered; this is not best handled, and too often, when a problem is discovered in the end, it is already too late either it takes an extended amount of time to locate where the problem originated from, or it becomes too costly and time-consuming to resolve the issue. Moreover, if an organization can regulate each dataset's data quality when it is gotten or made, the data quality is usually ensured. There are seven vital strides to accomplishing this necessary outcome.

Careful data profiling and control of approaching data

As a rule, terrible data originates from data getting. In an association, the data ordinarily originates from external sources outside the organization or office's control. It could be the data sent from another association, or, as a rule, gathered by outsider programming. This way, its data quality can't be guaranteed, and a complete data quality control of approaching data is undoubtedly the most significant perspective among all data quality control assignments. A decent data profiling instrument at that point proves to be handy; such a device ought to be fit for analyzing the accompanying parts of the data:

Data format and data patterns

Data consistency on each record

Data value distributions and abnormalities

Completeness of the data

It is also important to mechanize data profiling and data quality alarms, so the nature of approaching data is reliably controlled and overseen at whatever point it is gotten — never accept an approaching data to be equivalent to expected without first profiling checks. Finally, each piece of incoming data should be regulated using the same standards and best practices. A centralized catalog and KPI dash control should be set up to record and monitor the data's quality accurately.

Cautious data pipeline outline to avoid duplicate data

Copy data can be any record that unintentionally shares data with another record in your showcasing data base. The most apparent type of copy data is a finished duplicate of another record. These are the most effortless to spot and generally happen while moving data between systems. When a copy data is made, it is likely out of sync and prompts various outcomes, with falling results all through numerous systems or databases. In conclusion, when a data issue arises, it becomes difficult or time-consuming to locate the root cause and resolve it.

For an organization to prevent this occurrence, a data pipeline must be clearly defined and carefully structured in data assets, data modeling, business rules, and architecture. Effective communication is also required to enhance and authorize data sharing inside the association, generally improving effectiveness and reducing any potential data quality issues brought about by data duplications. This gets into the center of data control. On a high level, three areas need to be established to prevent duplicate data from being created:

A data oversight program clearly defining the ownership of a dataset and effectively communicates and promotes dataset sharing to prevent any department silos.

Centralized data assets management and data modeling, which are reviewed and audited consistently.

Straightforward, logical design of data pipelines at the enterprise level, which is shared across the organization.

With today's rapid technology platforms, solid data management, and enterprise-level data governance are essential for future successful platform migrations.

Accurate gathering of data requirements

The most crucial aspect of having good data quality is to assuage the requirements and deliver the data to clients and users for the original intent of the data. It isn't as basic as it first sounds, reason being:

It is difficult to introduce the data appropriately. To comprehend what a customer is searching for requires careful data revelations, data examination, and exact correspondences, regularly using data models and representations.

The prerequisite should include all data conditions and situations — it is viewed as fragmented if all the conditions or conditions are not evaluated and recorded.

With simple access and sharing, away from the necessities is another significant angle, which ought to be implemented by the Data Governance Committee.

The function of a Business Analyst is basic in necessity gathering. Their comprehension of the customers, just as current systems, permits them to communicate in the two sides' dialects. In the wake of get-together, the necessities, business investigators also perform sway examination and think of the test intends to ensure that the data delivered meets the prerequisites.

Enforcing data integrity

A significant feature of the relational database is enforcing data Integrity using methods such as foreign keys, check constraints, and triggers. It isn't as essential as it first sounds, reason being:

It is hard to present data suitably. To truly grasp what a client is looking for requires cautious data disclosures, data assessment, and exact correspondences, routinely by methods for data models and portrayals.

The essential should incorporate all data conditions and circumstances — it is seen as divided if all the conditions are not assessed and recorded.

With basic access and sharing, away from the necessities is another critical point, which should be actualized by the Data Governance Committee.

The capacity of a Business Analyst is fundamental in need assembling. Their cognizance of the clients, similar to current systems, licenses them to convey in the different sides' lingos. In the wake of get-together the necessities, business agents also perform influence assessment and consider test plans to ensure that the data conveyed meets the requirements. Data traceability is a bit more complicated than meta-data traceability. Underneath records some regular strategies used to empower this capacity:

Follow by interesting keys of each dataset: This initially requires each dataset has one or a gathering of one of a kind keys, which is then helped down to the downstream dataset through the pipeline. Also, only one out of every odd dataset can be situated by interesting keys. For instance, when a dataset is totaled, the source's keys get missing in the amassed data. Building a unique sequence number, such as transaction identifier or record identifier when unique keys in the data itself are not obvious

Building join tables when there are many-to-numerous connections, yet not 1-to-1or 1-to-many.

Include timestamp (or form) to every data record, to imply when it is included or changed

Log data change in a log table with the incentive before a change and the timestamp when the change is implemented

Information recognizability sets aside some effort to plan and actualize. Besides, it is deliberately basic for data modelers and architects to incorporate it with the pipeline from the earliest stage; it is verifiably worth the exertion thinking of it. It will spare a gigantic measure of time when a data quality issue occurs. Moreover, data recognizability lays the framework for improving data quality reports and dash controls that empower users to discover data before conveying the data to customers or interior clients.

Robotized relapse testing as a component of progress the control

Information quality issues frequently happen when another dataset is presented, or a current dataset is adjusted. For a successful change the executives, test plans ought to be worked with two topics: 1) affirming the change supplements the prerequisite

2) guaranteeing the change doesn't unintentionally affect the pipelines' data that should not be changed. For mission-basic datasets, when a change occurs, ordinary relapse testing should be executed for each deliverable, and correlations should be accomplished for each field and each column of a dataset. Seeing the quick improvement of technologies in massive data, framework relocation reliably occurs in a couple of years. Mechanized relapse test with careful data correlations is essential to ensure excellent data quality is looked after continually.

Competent data quality control groups

At last, two kinds of groups assume significant parts to guarantee high data quality for an association:

Quality Assurance: This group surveys the nature of programming and projects at whatever point modifications occur. Thorough change the executives performed by this group is of most extreme significance to guarantee data quality in an association that goes through quick changes and severe data applications.

Creation Quality Control: Depending on an association, this group doesn't need to be a different group without anyone else. It tends to be a component of the Quality Assurance or Business Analyst group Once in a while. The group needs to have a decent comprehension of the business rules and business prerequisites and be prepared by the instruments and dash controls to recognize variations from the norm, exceptions, broken patterns, and other strange situations in Production. This group's target is to distinguish any data quality issue and fix it before clients and customers do. This group also needs to band together with client care groups and get immediate criticism from clients and rapidly address their interests. With the advances of present-day AI advances, productivity can be conceivably improved radically. Notwithstanding, as expressed toward the start of this article, quality control toward the end is essential yet not adequate to guarantee an organization makes and supports excellent data quality. The six stages expressed above are additionally required.

Why Data Quality Matters

Helpless data quality can cost an association $10million yearly. Starting in 2016, it cost the United States $13 trillion every year. Information quality issues bring about a 20% lessening in laborer efficiency and clarify why 40% of business activities neglect to accomplish set objectives. Inaccurate data can hurt an association's notoriety, mislead assets, hinder data recovery, and lead to pseudo bits of knowledge and botched chances.

For example, if an association has a planned customer's false name or postage data, their advertising materials could go to an inappropriate beneficiary. On the off chance that business data is credited to an inappropriate SKU or brand, the organization may put resources into a product offering with the not precisely heavenly client request.

Indeed, blunders with data revealing have even brought about worldwide fiascoes. The Enron embarrassment of 2001, which came about because of the non-divulgence of billions of dollars of liabilities and prompted the vitality company's chapter 11, could have been forestalled through more exact reviewing that would have distinguished the manufactured idea of introduced data. Data quality matters all the time, but specific business contexts require extra extraordinary consideration paid to the data quality. While participating in a merger and obtaining, organizations need to bind together differentiating data sources under regular data norms, measures, procedures, advances, and societies. Information quality is additionally of a need for any undertaking asset arranging or client relationship the control work.

How you can preserve data quality

One of the essential duties of a data investigator is to ensure data quality. Either worker or client data passage can bring about information issues messes up (the most intermittent reason, as indicated by the data warehousing infrastructure), framework changes, programming blunders, or wrong data joining/relocation.

The strategy of analyzing data for precision and culmination is called data profiling. Information quality confirmation involves eliminating anomalies and breakdowns with the goal that the data is illustrative of the bigger picture.

The primary step in data profiling is making sure there are no missing data fields and that data has been correctly inputted.

The absolute most reoccurring issues influencing data quality are irregularity in designing dates and numbers, bizarre character sets and images, copy sections, and various dialects and estimation units. For example, a date can be worked out or spoken to mathematically in a couple of multiple organizations—dd/mm/yy, mm/dd/yy, or "day, month, the year"— which would impede a PC framework from precisely totaling and combining data identifying with time. Numerous associations use Unicode (general code principles) for data handling. In some cases, strange characters come through in a cluttered organization and must be changed over during the data purifying cycle.

After bringing in the data and featuring an issue, data examiners can either acknowledge the blunder if it doesn't disturb the understanding, eliminate the mistake, fix the error, or include a default, for example, "N/An" or "obscure" instead of the error.

When profiling enormous volumes of data, data investigators would expect data investigators to develop data chains of importance, rules, and term definitions to comprehend the interrelationships between data types. Rules can be straightforward; for example, "Full Customer name must be promoted and comprise of letters as it were." Data profiling checks what level of passages meet the guidelines and that this rate is over the edge required by the association.

Most times, issues relating to data can be fixed quite easily. For instance, inserting a drop-down menu into a survey instead of relying on free-form responses can enhance data consistency. Likewise, making mandatory fields reduces incomplete data occurrences, and requiring picture capture or GPS location and time stamp can improve data accuracy.

Associations with excellent data quality practices will have a cycle for mechanizing data assortment and passage (since various slips up caused are followed following to human mix-up), client profiles characterizing who ought to have the option to get to multiple data types, and a dash control to screen data quality changes after some time.

Information Quality Management

Information quality administration (DQM) alludes to a business rule that requires a mix of the correct individuals, cycles, and developments. The shared objective of improving the proportions of data quality that issues most to an undertaking association. That last part is significant: a definitive motivation behind DQM isn't merely to enhance the quality of data for having meaningful data but to accomplish the business results that rely on excellent data. The huge one is client relationship, control, or CRM. As regularly referred to, "CRM systems are just comparable to the data they contain."

A Foundation for High-Quality Data

Powerful data quality administration requires an auxiliary center that can uphold data tasks. These are four infrastructural standards to actualize significant data inside your data framework

Hierarchical Structure

IT initiative ought to consider the accompanying jobs while executing DQM rehearses over the venture:

DQM Program Manager: This job establishes the pace of data quality and sets up data quality necessities. The person being referred to is responsible for keeping a thought regarding ordinary data quality organization tasks, guaranteeing the group is on time, inside spending plan, and fulfilling foreordained data quality guidelines.

Association Change Manager: This individual is instrumental in the change the executives move that happens when data is utilized adequately; they settle on choices about data framework and cycles.

Information Analyst I or Business Analyst: This individual deciphers and reports on data.

Information steward: The data steward is accused of overseeing data as a corporate resource.

Information Profiling Audits

Information profiling is a review cycle that guarantees data quality. During this cycle, evaluators search for approval of data against meta-data and existing measures. At that point, they report on the nature of data. Directing data profiling exercises regularly is a specific method to guarantee your data is the quality expected to keep your association in front of the opposition

Information Reporting and Monitoring

For most associations, this alludes to the way toward checking, revealing, and recording exemptions. These exemptions can be caught by business knowledge (BI) programming for mechanized arrangements that capture terrible data before it gets usable.

Revising Errors

When conceivably terrible or fragmented data has been sifted through by BI systems, it's an ideal opportunity to make fitting data adjustments, for example, finishing the data, eliminating copies, or tending to some other data issue.

Five Best Practices for Data Quality Management

For organizations beginning the data quality administration measure, here are five accepted procedures to remember:

#1 Review Current Data

You probably have a great deal of client data, regardless. However, you would prefer not to throw it out and begin once again, as is commonly said in the tech world, "trash in, trash out."

What you should not do is fill your new data infrastructure with awful experiences. This way, when you're beginning with data quality administration, do a review of your present data; this includes taking stock of irregularities, blunders, copies; also, recording and altering any issues you run over to guarantee that the data that goes into your foundation is as high-bore as it might be.

#2 Data Quality Firewalls

A firewall is a mechanized cycle that forestalls and obstructs a representative fire. For this situation, the fire is awful data. Setting up a firewall to secure your association against terrible data will help keep the structure away from an error.

Client mistake is simple, and firewalls help forestall this cycle by hindering terrible data at the purpose of a passage. The number of individuals permitted to take care of data into the framework, to a great extent, influences the nature of the data. However, in numerous huge associations, it's basic to have different sections focuses.

A firewall assists data with staying mistake-free in any event when there are a few people with admittance to enter data.

#3 Integrate DQM with BI

In the present business culture, the buzz is about coordination; there isn't any valid reason why it shouldn't.

At the point when systems cooperate, they work better. The thought here is that no endeavor organization can legitimize the stores expected to search every data record for precision. Be that as it may, coordinating the DQM cycle with BI programming can assist with computerizing it. Given foreordained boundaries, certain datasets can be segregated for a survey; for example, new data collections that will probably be gotten to frequently can be inspected as a significant aspect of the DQM cycle.

#4 Put the Right People in Place

As portrayed above, there are a few situations inside your association responsible for the data quality cycle. Guaranteeing these positions are situated and committed to the activity implies ensuring administration guidelines can be met reliably.

#5 Ensure Data Governance with a Board

Making a data administration control shields organizations from the danger of settling on data-driven choices. The control should comprise of business and IT clients and heads. The gathering will set the arrangements and guidelines that become the infrastructure of data administration.

Likewise, the data administration control should meet intermittently to set new data quality objectives and screen the accomplishment of DQB activities DQM over the different LOB's, and this is the place building up a target estimation scale proves to be useful since to improve data quality, there must be an approach to gauge it.

Tools Needed For Data Quality Management

With the current technological development, organizations employ many tools to improve data quality, relating to their needs and preferences (cloud-put together versus concerning preface, a similarity with various sources, mixes with different stages, and data intricacy indexes).

These devices regularly perform three principal capacities: data purifying, data reviewing, and data relocation. Information examining has further developed capabilities than data cleansing and checks for extortion and other consistency weaknesses. Information movement includes moving different data collections to a data distribution center or brought together data index for capacity and data quality analysis.

Some mainstream programming services incorporate

Informatica is one of the most mainstream data the control programming alternatives. It accompanies many prebuilt data managers, a standard manufacturer for customization, and computerized reasoning (AI) abilities for diagnosing issues.

Talend has metadata the executive's arrangement and a mainstream device for the ETL (extricate, change, and burden) work. The essential bundle is free and open-source and gives a graphical portrayal of execution on consistency matters.

SAS The SAS data, the executive's device handles huge data volumes. Information quality technology is completely coordinated inside a similar design and can associate with different SAS tools for data perception and business examination

Prophet offers an assortment of data quality projects, including Oracle Big Data Cloud, Oracle Big Data Cloud Service, Oracle Big Data SQL Cloud Service, and Oracle NoSQL Database.

SAP – SAP HANA is an in-memory stage and database that recovers and stores data for applications.

IBM has a couple of various items, for example, the InfoSphere Data Server for Data Quality, to screen and purge data, investigate data for consistency, and make a comprehensive perspective on substances and connections.

The Future Of Data Quality

Information analysis is developing, and data quality norms must change. Progressively, governments are controlling data to guarantee morals and security through enactment like the General Data Protection Regulation in the European Union. With the rise of normal language preparing, AI, and computerized reasoning, the stakes for helpless data quality are higher. When utilizing past X-beam pictures to prepare machines to identify infections, it is fundamental that they are "learning" on clean data records or have hazardous outcomes. Since 60% of organizations refer to data quality as a hindrance for AI appropriation, data quality interest can cultivate a more AI-accommodating condition.

Advances in computerized reasoning can improve data quality via robotizing data catch, distinguishing abnormalities, and wiping out copies all the more rapidly; this will spare human time and consider more productive preparation of tremendous data indexes.

In seeking a vocation as a data investigator, data researcher, business expert, or data engineer, it is necessary to comprehend what establishes great data. Business results must be as useful as their data foundation.

Estimating Data Quality

Estimations of data quality are commonly planned to evaluate data quality components as characterized in the past area. As an initial step, a system must be set up with the pointers to assess. Next, an appropriate reference for confirmation of the data inside the data systems must be resolved.

Preferably, the data are looked at utilizing actual data, which considers approval and, whenever required, quick restorative activities. This technique is named data examining and is the main method of estimating the quality degree of extents like precision, fulfillment. Moreover, by experiencing the data itself, one can find data quality issues that were a sudden and special incentive for taking therapeutic measures to improve data quality. Notwithstanding, data evaluation comes at a significant expense as it is very tedious, and the requirement for specialists in the individual field is required.

Moreover, data examining can likewise be very work concentrated and necessitates that data regulators approach the actual data.

For example, consider the metadata of distributions that are contained in distributed databases. If a data regulator approves the metadata fields' substance with the metadata demonstrated on the distributions, mistakes can be distinguished. These can contain typical blemishes like spelling blunders yet can likewise give significant data on surprising errors that may be profoundly pertinent regarding the bibliometric analysis.

Data regulators can utilize rule-based checking to decide data quality on the off chance that the conditions for data inspecting are not met. This strategy intensely depends on business choices that are drafted depending on the data and experience the data regulators have regarding the data. Subsequently, these principles can just check for blemishes that were foreseen by the data regulators. Be that as it may, rule-based checking likewise offers significant points of interest, particularly as they can be computerized after transformation to approval rules, which considers the blunders (or conceivably right anomalies!) using data mining methods. The assumed errors actually should be amended, which remains work concentrated.

Significance of data quality

Normally, it isn't challenging to get everybody in the business, including the high-level administration, to concur that having excellent data quality is useful. In the current computerized change, the help for zeroing in on data quality is shockingly better than it was previously.

Notwithstanding, with regards to the fundamental inquiries concerning who is answerable for data quality, who must take care of business, and who will subsidize the essential exercises, at that point, circumstances become truly difficult.

Information quality takes after human wellbeing. Precisely testing how any one component of our eating routine and practicing may influence our wellbeing is mischievously troublesome. Similarly, strictly testing how any one piece of our data may affect our business is monstrously troublesome as well.

Innumerable encounters give us why terrible data quality isn't useful for business

In advertising, you overspend and irritate your possibilities by sending a similar material more than once to a similar individual – with the name and address spelled somewhat unique. The issue here is copies inside a comparable database and over a few inward and outside sources.

In online deals, you can't present adequate item data to help a self-administration purchasing choice. The issues here are the culmination of item data inside your data sets and how item data is partnered between exchanging accomplices.

In the graceful chain, you can't computerize measures dependent on concrete area data. The difficulties here are utilizing similar norms and include the vital exactness inside the area data.

In monetary detailing, you find various solutions for a similar inquiry because of conflicting data, shifting newness of data, and indistinct data definitions.

On a corporate level, data quality issues drastically affect meeting center business targets, as:

Failure to ideal respond to new market openings and consequently blocking benefit and development accomplishments. Regularly, this is expected not to be prepared for repurposing existing data that fit the previous prerequisites.

Hindrances in executing cost decrease programs, as the data must help the continuous business measures, need an excess manual review and amendment. Mechanization will just chip away at complete and reliable data.

Weaknesses in meeting expanding consistence necessities. These prerequisites range from security and data insurance guidelines as GDPR, wellbeing, and security necessities in different businesses to budgetary limitations, prerequisites, and rules. Better data quality is, on most occasions, an unquestionable requirement to meet those consistent destinations.

Troubles in abusing prescient examination on corporate data resources bringing about more danger than would generally be appropriate when making both present moment and long haul choices. These difficulties come from issues around duplication of data, data deficiency, data irregularity, and data incorrectness

Information Quality Reporting

Data profiling discoveries can be utilized to gauge data quality KPIs dependent on the data quality measurements pertinent to a given association. The discoveries from data coordinating are particularly helpful for estimating data uniqueness.

Notwithstanding that, it is useful to work a data quality issue log, where known data quality issues are recorded, and the preventive and data purifying exercises are followed up.

Associations zeroing in on data quality think that it is valuable to work a data quality dash control featuring the data quality KPIs and the pattern in their estimations just as the pattern in issues experiencing the data quality issue log.

CHAPTER FIVE - DATA ENGINEERING ON GOOGLE CLOUD

When it comes to ICT, data is an age-long-discussed subject that has been developed upon as the years go by. In understanding this subject's totality, we shall categorically discuss the key terms as our guide to the promised land.

MEANING OF DATA: data are statistics, facts, characters or symbols as the case may be, collected together for reference or analysis. Most people see data as raw data, and some say it is bare facts, while most others say it is unprocessed data.

From a more analytical perspective, data means a comprehensive group of symbols, words, letters, characters, etc. awaiting processing.

Data is the primary base and bedrock of all ICT related processes. The word mentor word reference considers data to be the amounts, characters, or images on which tasks are performed by a PC, which might be put away and communicated as electrical signals and recorded on attractive tape, optical, or mechanical chronicle media.

ENGINEERING: engineering is a branch of science that deals with buildings, engines, machines, and structures to achieve a predetermined goal. Engineering has many facets ranging from the electronics, to civil, to petroleum down to ICT.

In this subject, engineering, as it relates to ICT, is our paramount discussion. Engineering simply is a systematic way of solving human problems to bring about a flexible and enjoyable life.

GOOGLE CLOUD: this is a platform on the web owned and managed by Google to provide an array of services to her costumers. According to Wikipedia, the Google cloud stage is a set-up of distributed computing services that sudden spikes in demand for a similar framework that Google utilizes inside for its end-client items, for example, Google search, Gmail, and youtube. Close by many control tools gives a progression of particular cloud services, including computing, data storage, data analysis, and AI.

DATA ENGINEERING ON GOOGLE CLOUD is a platform created by Google that helps participants to effectively plan and assemble data preparing systems on the cloud platform through a careful combination of presentation, demonstration, and practice.

The practice of data engineering on Google cloud is so visible that it is advisable that those who seek to practice this act must be armed with the prerequisites.

Any Google cloud participant or the user should be conversant with some basic query languages such as SQL. Such participants should have experience in extracting, loading, transforming, cleaning, and validating data, designing core pipelines and architecture for data processing, integrating analytics and machine learning abilities into data pipelines, computing and visualizing query querying data sets, and creating results.

BASIC REQUIREMENTS FOR PARTICIPANTS ON GOOGLE CLOUD.

- Every participant should have completed some Google cloud fundamentals example, the big data, and machine learning course or at least have an equivalent in knowledge

- Should be proficient with the query languages which an example is SQL

- Should know about developing an application using standard programming languages such as python
- Should be conversant and familiar with machine or statistics
- It should be experienced with data modeling, extract, transform, and load activities.

THE PROCESS OF STORING AND ANALYSING YOUR DATA IN GOOGLE CLOUD.

Pop-up stickers were often averring the need for more computers and a robust network through a high-performance super-fast network. The good news is this, the same provisions that can provide you with all that; supper fast access, quick response times, and reliability that Google uses to index the web, search results, run Google mail and a larger scale of possibilities is made available on your platform for your application. Google cloud drive gives users opportunities to manage and access all their file content in the Google cloud and reach it anywhere. It is worthy to note that while Google drives enables a platform for uploading files, searching and retrieving stored items through the vapi produced by Google

Google Cloud Storage allows developers and users to store and keep their data in Google's cloud. Google Cloud Storage is suited initially to act as a content repository having an unlimited number of files and documents of whatsoever size that can be shared with anybody and speedily accessed by such individuals. For example, one pharmaceutical industry uses it to store the list of drugs present, the sales they have made, their profits, and even the names and salary scale of their workers.

It is also used for all sorts of data back up and accessing archived data and data speedily. A cheap option is available for archiving data that does not need continuous speedy retrieval access. In most cases,

Google Cloud Storage acts as the intermediary storage facility for other services in the Google Cloud Platform. For example, it serves as the center service for Google Cloud SQL and Big Question to get to data from different systems and fare data to other systems in like manner. You don't make data in Cloud Storage as it is now existent. You just store the vital existing data in Google Cloud Storage. You can upload and download necessary documents:

- interactively using the online browser
- from a command line using the gsutil tool or any other tool of choice strategically using Google Cloud Storage's REST API to add, to simply uploading or downloading data as the case may be.

You can also serve content via HTTP directly from Google Cloud Storage. For instance, one can create a hyperlink or even paste a URL into a program's location bar. Google Cloud Storage presents the substance in a profoundly flexible and superb manner. You can even serve whole static sites from Google Cloud Storage, and it will show up sensibly.

GOOGLE CLOUD STORAGE API. Google Cloud Storage uses buckets to contain materials and objects, where a bucket is similar to a directory, and an item or material is identical to a file or folder. The Google Cloud Storage API provides an internet web interface for making HTTP requests to work with buckets and materials or articles. The Google Cloud Storage API upholds HTTP strategies for Listing buckets, Creating and erasing wanted buckets, doctoring and listing who can access these so-called buckets, Uploading and downloading objects, Deleting objects in a bucket, Uploading items using HTML forms, amongst many other available services that can be achieved on the platform.

Google Cloud SQL. This Google platform SQL allows you to create, configure, and use the SQL databases inherent in Google cloud. It is a fully managed service that maintains and manages your databases. Google Cloud SQL is intended for programming use within applications. It has a core interactive UI that helps learn about the product and further services offered thereupon. Beginning, using it, investigating the various schema, and submitting essential trial queries. My SQL is a full interactional database system that supports full SQL syntax and table management tools. Google Cloud SQL supports a subset of My SQL, which includes most of My SQL features. For a list of essential differences, it is necessary to see the Google Cloud SQL FAQ. Generally, Google Cloud SQL is good for randomly small or medium sets of data:

- must be kept consistent
- are updated frequently
- are queried often in many different ways, amid-st other characters for consideration.

Google Cloud SQL is generally used for data administration rather than data analysis only; it encourages updating, correcting, and deleting queries and so many other functions. Concretely put in database terms, Google Cloud SQL is an OLTP web transaction processing system.

And its exact uses include keeping track and record of user orders, product catalogs, discussion controls and blogs, concrete content management systems, and workflow applications.

Google Cloud SQL allows its user to import the databases of choice or create them new. SQL users can perform the usually required SQL directives to assembling and drop database tables, and to make, improve, and erase columns and data as follows:

- intuitively from the online SQL brief

- from the order line with the Google SQL device
- from App Engine applications and devices
- efficiently from different applications utilizing JDBC
- from Apps Scripts of content
- using outsider devices, for example, the Squirrel SQL customer.

IMPORTING AND EXPORTING DATA

To import databases from other My SQL databases, you have first to copy the data, whether as a file or documentary or in any format, to Google Cloud Storage and thereupon import it from there into Google Cloud SQL.

On the other hand, to export your data from there, you use the Export option in the Google Cloud console to export your desired data to Google Cloud Storage as the case may be.

BIGQUERY the Google BIGQUERY Service is an ultra-large parallel query data store that allows you to run SQL like queries against very large data sets, with potentially uncountable rows in a matter of seconds and minutes depending on the size of the documentary in general. It is intended for programmatic use within applications and thus provides an interactive UI, which helps learn about the product and run interactive queries pari pasu.

BIGQUERY is embedded in Google's essential technologies and has been used internally by Google and her users for various analytical tasks since 2006, wherefrom up to this current year. BIGQUERY backs analysis of data sets up to hundreds of terabytes and beyond and so on. To effectively use BIGQUERY, you upload your choice data into BIGQUERY, and then you can query it interactively or programmatically. You can also query publicly available data sets and data sets that other people wished and shared with you. There are ways one can use BIGQUERY under various circumstances:

- interactively through the BIGQUERY browser tool
- using the BIGQUERRY command-line tool
- programmatic-ally by making essential calls to the REST API using various client libraries in multiple languages, such as Java and Python.

EXAMPLES OF USED CASES. BIGQUERY is best for the running queries over vast amounts of data up to billions of rows in s short time. It is suitable for analyzing large quantities of data quickly, but not for modifying it. In data analyzing terms, BIGQUERY is an online analytical processing system and works best for interactive analysis of large data sets, regularly utilizing a few huge, attach just tables. One explicit model utilization of BIGQUERY is by Red Bus, an online travel service that acquainted Internet transport tagging with India in 2006. Utilizing BIGQUERY, they dissected the client head out the movement to recognize which courses required more transports, where new transport courses were required, and whether diminished appointments on explicit courses were brought about by worker issues or essentially by less interest. As per Pradeep Kumar, the creator of their specialized contextual investigation, "We had a table which contained 2tera byte of data yet returned inquiry results in less than 30 seconds for most inquiries." through this examination, it is just clear that the effectiveness level of the big question is on the high side.

CREATION OF DATA AND INGESTION IN BIG QUERRY.

BIGQUERY can import data through the following methods:

i. THE CSV PLATFORM. It is an essential tool with a relatively simple, compact format for flat data structures.

ii. THE JSON TOOL is more of a concrete format that symbolizes finished and repeated data. Moreover, it is easily parsed identifiable by both humans and code.

iii. APPLICATION ENGINES STORES DATA IN BACKUPS; Up to 500 source files and data can be ingested in a single batch, with the largest possible intake 1TeraByte of the total data per load job as of in Jan 2013. presently now very little has changed.

BIGQUERY Can Import Data From These Various Platforms:

the Google Cloud Storage

The Local files on your computer

Microsoft Excel and its likes

The various Third-party systems using available third-party tools such as Pervasive, Knime, or Informatics as the case may be.

BIGQUERY Does The Following Ways To Import existing data Data:

i. Interactively via the BIGQUERY UI

ii. Using the BIGQUERY command-line tool

iii. Programmatic-ally making use of the REST API tool

iv. Making Use of the Excel connector

v. Working with the other tools discussed here upon inside this document.

USING THE BIG QUERY MODEL TO UPLOAD DATA. One can use the UI online to upload data and data files in your computer machine or from the Google cloud storage strategically. One can also export data in the same vein, which are query results as a CSV file to your computer or instead as a permanent table, your data set. One can also export an entire data set table to the Google cloud unit of storage from the big query UI.

There are two strategic ways one can effectively upload source data into Google BIGQUERY; these are

Such individual making such importation from local files

Or the same individual is importing such files from the Google cloud storage bucket.

It will only be relatively easy if such data files are small and from a single source file. Google cloud storage is the best to stage data files for a big query. One major benefit of its use, I mean Google cloud storage bucket, is that the source files can be kept thereupon as an archive as it will be more convenient if there are still intentions to ingest such files back into the platform.

HOW THE THIRD PARTY TOOLS VISUALIZE AND INGEST DATA

These third-party tools in their numbers provide and effectively take care of importing and visualizing data into the big query. There are a lot of these tools used for business intelligence and visualizing, and some of them are as follows;

JASPER SOFT. This tool has co-joined its business intelligence product with the BIGQUERY

QLIK VIEW. On this system, the custom connector that helps pull data into their in-memory data for structuring is provided

BIME ANALYTICS. This one provides the necessary connection that allows online immediate querying from the BIGQUERY with an interactive data analysis dash control

MATRIC INSIGHTS. In the BI platforms, this tool offers the BIGQUERRY plugging

TABLEAU. This field offers a direct connection to BIGQUERRY for visualizing data.

SOME OF THE BASIC ETL TOOLS.

These basic tools required for uploading data into the BIGQUERY are as follows

INFORMATICA. It has with it a cloud connector for the Google BIGQUERY and Google cloud storage

PERVASIVE. This one provides a permanent solution for the rush analyzer tool that allows BIGQUERY to be utilized as an output writer for any workflow.

TALEND. This tool gives continuous support for the BIGQUERY right in an open studio for large data files, an open-source set of code generation tools to structure and execute data generation.

SQL SREAM. It provides a continuous ETL connector for the BIGQUERY. It happens that when data or data flows into the SQL stream in a specific pattern, it is immediately queued for inserting into the BIGQUERRY on a continuous recurring basis. It is of tangent necessity that one knows when to use the BIGQUERY or the

Google cloud SQL; this is necessary because places in which they are to e used vary.

The BIGQUERY allows you to import substantial quantities of data and, at the same time, perform scrutiny function on it. On the other hand, Google Cloud SQL will enable you to host an MYSQL relational database in Google's cloud and, at the same time, design, create and update your tales and rows directly.

OLAP COMPARED TO OLTP

While OLTP means an online analytical processing tool, the OLTP is the online transaction processing tool. Both of them are all tools used for both analyzing and processing data. The BIG QUAL falls under the online analytical processing tool because it is built for processing data only in batches. On the other side is the Google cloud SQL that falls under the online transaction processing (OLTP), and it supports high volume and low latency queries in real-time.

DATA PROCESSING ABILITIES.

Big query wields the core ability to process huge terabytes of data in a very speedy and fast manner. Simultaneously, on this other side, Google Cloud SQL has a limited number of just a hundred gigabytes per database. Presently there have been some improvements, but these improvements are not far from the above-written texts.

BIG QUERY AND DATA MODIFICATIONS

The BIG QUERY tool cannot in any way enhance or doctor available data that has already been posted on the BIG QUERY TABLE. Meanwhile, with the Google Cloud SQL, you are given full control over enhancing and doctoring the said data on the same BIG QUAL TABLE.

THE APPLICATION ENGINE DATA STORE.

The application Engine is a Service platform; it is usually called platform as a service (PaaS).

It provisions an SDK and the necessary tools for developing intended applications on Python and Java. Application Engine is systems for developing speedily, highly scalable internet applications that run atop Google's infrastructure. As the traffic con-gesture to your application enlarges, more clones of your application are created immediately to handle the loads, allowing your application to increase managing millions of people using such a platform. The Application Engine provisions an SDK systematically to help you enhance your applications.

Subjects of discussing under this platform are so vast, so this piece will be focusing on how to store data, and if to use the built-in data store or if better still, for the Application Engine to make use of Google Cloud SQL or Google Cloud Storage to save its data. To improve more on your knowledge about App Engine practicals and constant practice is required

It is also important that one understands what data is important and is of relative importance to the subject of discussion.

Application Engine Datastore is an analytical storage system used to store data used in and generated by the Engine applications

To effectively query and store data in the datastore space, you write in the accepted codes in any of the languages supported by the Application Engine.

The Datastore is a non-relational value store that supports scaling in its unlimited forms; this means one can store any value pairs of data you want. All the characters stored in the Datastore does not need to fit into the same structure.

The Datastore safe keeps the data on Google's infrastructure the same way that Google stores its data, such as the key-value pairs that stand in for indexed values for all the web pages that Google runs and manages.

One can also make use of the Mem-cache service to keep the data values right in the cache to reduce stress to the datastore

THE ACT OF QUERYING THE DATASTORE

Application Engine knowledge store permits you to store knowledge as key valued pairs any observed as entities. These entity characters area unit indexed and may be queried. Therefore, the application Engine provisions associate degree API for querying the data on the data store in Python and Java. Though the question API does not provide SQL's big question practicality, it's consistently optimized for the data store materials' schema-less format. Therefore permitting you to line your filters and models for looking for materials and entities. Hereupon there's conjointly a SQL querying language known as GQL that's syntactically synonymous to SQL solely that it implements a set of the desired practicality

THE ADMINISTRATIVE CONSOLE.

The App Engines body console provides insight into the hold on knowledge. It permits you to run GQL queries within the knowledge store read panels, which may be of large quality for directors to interrogate, petition, question, and restore meant stored-up knowledge.

USING THE APP ENGINE KNOWLEDGE STORE OR THE GOOGLE CLOUD STORAGE UNITS.

The Google Cloud Storage is intentional to host write-once knowledge, wherever within the knowledge store is for ma-liable application knowledge and data. Note that for often sterilization key valued pairs, place the data store to use. Usually |this can be} due to a significant amount of data that will not be altered often like existing documents and radical massive binary files conjointly referred to as blobs, use the Google Cloud Storage platform.

The Application Engine will use the Google Cloud Storage concretely as a passage for knowledge distribution with customers outside the application's jurisdiction. Then if your knowledge afore exists as files on the far side the applying Engine, the structural resolution is to transfer it to the Google Cloud Storage and pull it thereupon it into your application. If your Application Engine generates massive amounts of knowledge that require be accessibility outside identical applications, store the data in Google Cloud Storage.

USING GOOGLE CLOUD STORAGE WITH APPLICATION ENGINE

To get to Google Cloud Storage, App Engine applications will either use the remainder API provided by Google Cloud Storage or use API the custom Application Engine Files.

the Application Engines custom API for storing and serving knowledge from the Google Cloud Storage service is a lot of direct and economical than the remainder protocol interface [Java API, Python API]

THE USE OF GOOGLE CLOUD SQL OR THE APP ENGINE KNOWLEDGE STORE

The App Engine knowledge store and Google Cloud SQL are accustomed to store identical applications and knowledge; however, the data store uses schema-less, No SQL knowledge, whereas the Google Cloud SQL stores knowledge in My SQL tables.

The App Engine Datastore provides NoSQL key-value storage that's extremely scalable. Google Cloud SQL supports advanced queries and ACID transactions; however, this suggests the info acts as a 'fixed pipe' and performance is a smaller amount scalable. The choice doubtless comes right down to whether or not you're more comfortable with ancient SQL with tightly-managed schema, or NoSQL wherever there are no necessities of conformity across objects of the identical kind. Several applications use each style of storage.

GOOGLE CALCULATE ENGINE

Google calculates Engine is associate degree Infrastructure as a Service (IaaS) giving that helps you run your large-scale computing workloads on UNIX system virtual machines hosted on Google's infrastructure. The applications' event is up to you to develop and run no matter the services and applications you wish. Your applications will use the Programming interface and guidance devices by Google Drive, Google Cloud Storage, Google Cloud SQL, and BigQuery to incorporate with data facilitated over the Google Cloud Platform.

Applications running on Google calculate Engine will store their application knowledge victimization one in every of the following::

- Persistent disk. It is a type of disc that can be a replicated, network-connected storage service equivalent to the latency and performance of native disks. Knowledge written to the present device is copied to multiple physical disks in an exceedingly Google knowledge center. You'll conjointly produce snapshots of your disks for backup/restore functions and may mount these devices in an exceeding mode that enables multiple virtual machines to scan from one device.
- Google Cloud Storage — simply access your Google Cloud Storage knowledge buckets from within a virtual machine.

The seamless authentication makes it simple to firmly access your knowledge while not managing keys in your virtual machines.

How To Chose Among The App Engine And Google Calculate Engine

App Engine may be a Platform as a Service (PaaS) service. It provides associate degree SDK and a collection of tools for developing applications in Java and Python severally. It gives modules to basic joining with the Eclipse development setting and accompanies layouts for running a "Welcome World" application directly out of the crate. The SDK provides standard code to making web applications and licenses you to send your applications with basically a click. You continue to write the logic of the applying, and however, when you've sent your application, Google keeps it running for you and imitates the data. You'll utilize App Engine to get started quickly developing and deploying an online application. However, you're affected by the supported languages and, therefore, the necessities of the framework.

Google calculates Engine, on the opposite hand, is associate degree Infrastructure as a Service (IaaS) giving. Google gives the framework to you to run your applications; be that as it may, you must style them, create them, if you wish them to e spot to keen use

CHAPTER SIX - PREPARING FOR A GOOGLE CLOUD EXAM

Google cloud confirmations are one of the most searched after IT accreditations everywhere in the world. It has gotten truly significant for any Data Engineer to get a Google Certification to advance in the IT business. As of late, Spotify has been building up an occasion conveyance framework on Google Cloud Platform. The cloud scene is getting extremely serious as far as valuing too for development in the business.

A data engineer working on a cloud platform also performs some other responsibilities such as analysis of data to draw insight and then converting them to the business outcomes, creating machine learning models for automating and simplifying the key business processes, and building statistical models for supporting decision-making said that 90% of the data had been made over the most recent two years. The development will proceed for the following five years. So every other IT organization is embracing Google Cloud, and for a Data Engineer, it has become a significant angle as a few positions are appearing.

So if you are going for Google cloud accreditation for Data Engineer, at that point, you should follow the right track for Google data engineer confirmation readiness.

This learning way is intended to help you get ready for the Google Certified Professional Data Engineer Exam. Regardless of whether you don't plan to take the test, these courses will help you increase a strong comprehension of the different data preparing segments of the Google Cloud Platform. At the core of Google's large data services is BigQuery, and oversaw data distribution center in the cloud. The initial three courses will tell you the best way to load and inquiry data in BigQuery, streamline BigQuery's exhibition, and imagine your data. The following three courses will tell you the best way to deal with your data.

First, you will utilize the Cloud Machine Learning Engine to prepare neural organizations to perform prescient examination. Next, you'll use Cloud Dataflow and Cloud Dataproc to manufacture data handling pipelines that change and sum up your data utilizing Apache Beam, Hadoop, and Spark. The last course will acquaint you with Bigtable, Google's progressive NoSQL database. The best way to exploit Bigtable's superior to huge data applications. These courses remember hands-for demos you can do yourself. At that point, you can test what you've realized by taking the training test.

Getting a Google Data Engineer accreditation is anything but a troublesome cycle; however, meaningfully affects your vocation and employment in the IT business. It has been a decent history with worth and advantages for workers and bosses, which incorporates: Our goal today is to help enable you to take the Google Cloud Data engineering exam and be successful the first time you take the exam. One area of focus around taking a Google exam is understanding where to study and how to study. As with any other vendor, you know, Google does a fairly decent job of trying to define what you have to study. It just sometimes isn't as clear as it could be. Now it's necessary to point out one area when we get to it that you definitely should want to study for the test a little more than what it would appear you would be tested on based on the GTA and demonstration areas go through. So what is a data engineer? Simply put, the Data engineer enables a data-driven decision approaching, and the goal is to collect, transform, and visualize data. The Data engineer would build a design, maintain and troubleshoot data processing scenarios, etc. this is just to make sure that we had a baseline to go through. The Google cloud data beta engineering exam is 100 questions, and the cost was $120. The exact time was four hours for the beta. When this goes into production, it'll likely be 50 questions, and you'll get about 90 minutes or two hours. I forgot exactly what the architect is now, but I see a metal follow the same path now. The main challenge with the test can sign up and take it, and this implies that they use a company called Criterion as their Test Proctor. If you're in a small city like Jacksonville, Des Moines, Savannah, you may be challenged to take this exam. And the reason is that its criterion has a limited number of proctoring centers based on statistics found. So, if you're in a bigger city of pride, this wouldn't be a problem, and this is weeks and weeks and weeks. So again, it's plausible to think that Criterion was not a good choice for a global company like Google. Having had the opportunity to develop many exams for different organizations, and worked with CompTIA, being the cloud subject matter expert on the cloud essentials and the first version of the CompTIA. Cloud plus exams. Also, having had the privilege of working for verkade on several of verkade certifications as well. So with that is the edge of having a fairly good knowledge of how test development should occur, and from observations, Google didn't spend or invest a lot of time in this area. So when you take the test, you are going to find grammatical errors likely. It's roughly spent about 15 minutes making comments to at least 16 or 17 questions around grammar or pronunciation or not pronunciation, but the way you write a question would be so obvious that probably someone that doesn't speak English as a primary language wrote it, and again, nothing wrong with that per se, but these are mistakes that clearly, if used to bloom system or some kind of other best practice with JT, Aizen, Test development, etc. You probably wouldn't have made. So the task again probably needed a little bit more reviewing. As far as case studies, Google listed the key studies and gave you the case studies you're going to see on the exam, so you had time to review the case studies before taking the exam. Now that's a beautiful thing, especially if your little tight on time, so you didn't have to like read into the exam three or four times to make sure you understood the case study and the scenarios they give you study. So at least that way, you had a heads up by reviewing the case study; that was a nice thing to do. Cloud Data Proc So here's the technical areas you're going to see on the task. DATA PROC knows what it is, know how to migrate it and migrate with it. For example, CloudData Flow numerous questions around Data Flow and know the difference between streaming and batching that were a couple of references to that. Know that it's a managed service. Also, know that you could use it for ETL too. Lastly, know that cloud data flow. You could also integrate and manage services with cloud storage as well as compute engines. So do understand how this all could work together. Pipelines this is another area that you might want to know also to question was asking about JSON or Java. How would you use it, and how could you? Choose one over another would be the primary focus for the pipeline, so do have a good idea around what Jason is in Java as well, of course. Storage now, this is fairly heavily tested. Overall, I thought they talked about cloud storage quite a bit. Also, know why you may want to use big data storage or cold line storage versus cloud storage, for example. Hadoop gets warm and fuzzy with the deep before you take the test. And here's why you're not going to get Hadoop, but you're going to get tested on others. Other solutions, like hives, scroup, oozie, as well as a peg and mapper someone I didn't let leave there and the reason is you going to get numerous questions on why you would want to use hive or would you use scroup or would use mapper or do you use? Um peg, for example. So, for example, if you're talking about ETL, know what you're going to use. If you're talking about. Processing data know what you're going to use, for example, reducing data, consolidating, etc. Just know what these services are. Also too there is a question on HC FS. Do you know what that is? OK now stack driver for those that don't know what it is, that driver is Googles Essentially monitoring service. It's considered a hybrid monitoring service. Even though I consider that more around operations than anything else, they wanted, not so much that you knew what Stackdriver was, but how you could use stack driver to be able to. Debug source code, for example, or how to monitor? Example applications and how to solve problems around troubleshooting with stack driver. Big table, big query cloud SQL know what these are, you will get tested heavily on these. Now understand what a big table is. Why would you use a big table over a big query? Know what it is, which ones have data warehouse? Which one is a new SQL database? Know those things and how you could tie them into cloud storage or how you could migrate data. As well as from a customer site as well. Cloud SQL, they want you to know about cloud SQL, it seemed like they tested more heavily on a big table and big query then cloud SQL, but if you're good at SQL, you're going to know cloud SQL fairly straightforward. Machine language, machine learning, and artificial intelligence. Now again, having known what those are, for me, I'm just not focused on those areas, so I don't have that super-rich experience around it. Now for the task. They're going to ask you about tensor flow in, and yes, we're going to ask you about Mandelbrot and cloud ML. Still, when you take the test, you're going to find that there is going to be you know somewhere probably around 10% of the test just on this area again you know you probably won't feel the test if you Again, you know you probably won't fill the test if you don't know it. If you know everything else. But again, this is tested heavily, and there are some new terms in there that I didn't know. What they're talking about, so this is an area I had to pass over pretty much now. Cloud lab cloud data lab. Now again, you need to know what this is. It seems like they wanted to know this falls under the big data realm where they wanted to make sure you know how to analyze transform, and it seemed most importantly, visualize the data. So they asked you about different solutions out there for visualizing data, what you could use. Also, they wanted to make sure you knew about the different models around data analysis as well, so get to know that. After taking the test, one thing to do is to do some further research on tensor flow and what Mandelbrot is and what a set is and dive into machine learning a little bit more than what you have experience with. To get to know what you need to know for the task is, Google has that documentation on the Google Cloud page, so again, you're going to need to know a little bit outside of what is a document on Google GCP that is, so read into this, you're going to do OK if you can understand a lot of terminologies. Now PubSub is Google's messaging service that you could tie in integrating with other services engine, this you'll get a couple questions on PubSub.

CHAPTER SEVEN - DATA ENGINEERING EXAMINATION

Data professionals on data engineering allow based and driven decision making by collecting, transforming, and publishing data. Once one is certified as a data engineer, he should build but design, operationalize, secure, and monitor data processing systems on compliance, reliability, fidelity, efficiency, malleability, and portability. The work of one who happens to be a data engineer should go beyond and to the extent of leveraging, deploying, and continuously training the existing and pre-existing models.

The professional engineering exam is an assessment of the individual involved to check and weigh such a person's abilities, capabilities, and strengths.

Building and operationalizing of data processing systems

Design and data processing systems

An operational machine learning model

Ensuring solution quality

This professional exam scales your abilities on whether you can build and operate data processing systems by giving you a list of tasks to be performed on the platform under limited time

They also go-ahead to provide you with ideas in which you are to bring to reality by designing such on the data processing system upon the Google cloud

They go to the very ends testing weather you can operate machine learning models, together with whether you have the efficient pro skills in managing all the fore mentioned aspects

After all these, they demand solutions to problems they make available, testing how quality assured the solution you would proffer comes out.

EXAMINATION LANGUAGES. For most people interested in these exams, these exams are written in English and japan languages. It only denotes that an individual should be acclimatized to one of them or both as the case may be.

EXAMINATION REGISTRATION. The current registration fee for registering for this exam stands at about $200 in addition to taxes where payable.

EXAMINATION TIME. The exams last for about two(2) hours or a little more length as the case may be.

EXAMINATION FORMAT. The exam is being served in two forms, which are multiple select and multiple choice. These exams are either taken remotely or by the person at the center. This entails that you need to locate the nearest center for proper registration to take this exam.

EXAMINATION SUBMITTING AND DELIVERY METHODS. It is advisable to take the online proctored exam from your remote location and review the online testing requirements.

The onsite-proctored examination is being taken at the testing center just as the name implies. To take this exam, one needs to locate the center nearest to him/her to accomplish this task

There are no prerequisites to take this examination

RECOMMENDATION AND EXPERIENCE FOR EXAMINATION. A three(3) year of industry experience is recommended, including a one-year designing and managing solutions using the GCP.

EXAMINATION GUIDE. It is customary to seek and stick with the examination guidelines and principles to excel in any examination test. This exam guide contains a given list of necessary knowledge before stepping into the exam arena. These topics may be added as examination questions. one must review the examination guide to make sure that his skills fall under the places of necessary discuss in the examination

EXAMINATION PRACTICE. While the exam tests technical skills that are mindful of the job role, hands-on experience is the best preparation for the exam. Most individuals feel the need more knowledge and skill for the examination or let alone practice; it is best to use the hands-on lab made available by quick labs or the GCP free tier to boost your skills and knowledge. Suppose one still feels that they are not yet in perfect shape for the exams. In that case, there are still preparatory classes and trial examinations still available on the platforms, as mentioned earlier.

CONCRETE ANALYSIS OF EXAMINATION GUIDE

Here is the list of all topics one needs to be conversant with upon entering the examination arena.

Designing data processing systems

Selecting the right storage technologies from the random many, which include:

Mapping storage systems to business requirements and needs

Data modeling

Trade-offs having to do with latency, throughput, transactions, and other transactions

Distributed systems

Scheme designs

1.2 Designing data pipelines. Considerations include:

Data publishing and visualization, an example is BigQuery(BQ).

Batch and streaming data is Cloud Data flow, Cloud Data proc, Apache Beam, Apache Spark and Hadoop ecosystem, Cloud Pub/Sub, Apache Kafka.

Online (communication/ interaction) vs. batch predictions

Job automation and orchestration an example Cloud Composer

1.3 Designing a data processing solution. Considerations include:

Choice of infrastructure

System availability and fault tolerance

Use of distributed systems

Capacity planning

Hybrid cloud and edge computing

Architecture options (e.g., message brokers, message queues, middleware, service-oriented architecture, server-less functions)

At least one after the other, etc., event processing

1.4 Migrating data warehousing and data processing. Considerations include:

Awareness of current state and how to migrate a design to a future state

Migrating from on-premises to cloud (Data Transfer Service, Transfer Appliance, Cloud Networking)

Validating a migration

2. Building and operationalizing data processing systems

2.1 Building and operationalizing the storage systems. The various considerations include:

Effective use of managed services (Cloud Big table, Cloud Spanner, Cloud SQL, Big Query, Cloud Storage, Cloud Datastore, Cloud Memory store)

Storage costs and performance

Life cycle management of data

2.2 Building and operationalizing pipelines. Considerations include:

Data cleansing

Batch and streaming

Transformation

data acquisition and import

integration with new data sources

2.3 Building and operationalizing process infrastructure. concerns include:

Provisioning resources

Ii. observance pipelines

Adjusting pipelines

Testing and internal control

3. Operationalizing machine learning models

3.1 leverage pre-engineered metric capacity unit models as a service. concerns include:

metric capacity unit arthropod genus (e.g., Vision API, Speech API)

Customizing metric capacity unit arthropod genus (e.g., AutoML Vision, car metric capacity unit text)

informal experiences (e.g., Dialogflow)

3.2 Deploying Associate in Nursing metric capacity unit pipeline. concerns include:

Ingesting acceptable data

preparation of machine learning models (Cloud Machine Learning Engine, massive question metric capacity unit, Kube flow, Spark ML)

Continuous analysis

3.3 selecting the acceptable coaching and serving infrastructure. concerns include:

Distributed vs. single machine

Use of edge figure

Hardware accelerators (e.g., GPU, TPU)

3.4 activity, monitoring, and troubleshooting machine learning models. the assorted concerns include:

Machine learning terminologies. Examples embody options labels, models, regression, classification, recommendation, supervised and unsupervised learning, analysis metrics

Impact of dependencies of machine learning models

Common sources of error presumptions of knowledge statistics

4. making certain resolution quality

4.1 coming up with for security and compliance. Major concerns include:

Identity and access management example Cloud IAM

data security example coding, key management

making specific privacy example data Loss bar API

Legal compliance example insurance movableness and answerability Act (HIPAA), Children's on-line Privacy Protection Act (COPPA), FedRAMP, General Data Protection Regulation (GDPR))

4.2 making certain measurability and potency. concerns include:

Building and running check suites

Pipeline observance example Stack driver

Assessing, troubleshooting, and raising data representations and processing infrastructure

Refiller and car scaling resources

4.3 making certain reliableness and fidelity. Major concerns include:

performing arts data preparation and internal control (e.g., Cloud data prep)

Verification and observance

Planning, executing, and stress testing data recovery (fault tolerance, rerunning failing jobs, performing arts retrospective re-analysis)

selecting between ACID, idempotent, eventually consistent needs

4.4 making certain flexibility and movableness. concerns include:

Mapping to current and future business needs

coming up with for data and application movableness (e.g., multi-cloud, data residency requirements)

data staging, cataloging, and discovery

For concrete examination, one must be acclimatized with all listed for achievement

CHAPTER EIGHT - CONCLUSION AND OUTLINE

Generally, Google Cloud is created from a collection of tangible assets, like computers, virtual resources, and fixed disk drives like virtual machines (VMs), that area unit contained in the Google data centers all around the world. Each data unit location is in a particular geographical jurisdiction. Such regions area unit is obtainable in Australia, North America, Europe, and Asia. Every region can have a set of zones, that area unit unbroken distant from one another all among the region. Every zonal unit is known unambiguously by a reputation that mixes the region's name with a letter symbol. As an example, zone C in the North America region is named America north 1c and different. This even distribution of resources provisions various advantages and redundancy just in case of failure and reduced latency by locating resources nearer to shoppers. This distribution additionally introduces some rules regarding; however, resources may be used along.

In cloud computing, what you may be accustomed to thinking of as computer code and hardware products, become services. These services offer access to the underlying resources. The list of available Google Cloud services is long, and it keeps growing. Once you develop your web site or application on Google Cloud, you combine and match these services into mixtures that offer the infrastructure you wish, and so add your code to change the eventualities you would like to make.

Other resources across regions and zones may access some resources. These global resources include pre-organized disk pictures, disk snapshots, and networks. Some resources may be accessed solely by resources that area unit placed within the same region. These regional resources include static external data processing addresses. Different resources may be accessed exclusively by resources that area unit placed within the same zone. These zonal resources include VM instances, their varieties, and disks.

The scope of associate degree operation varies, looking at what reasonably resources you are operating with. As an example, making a network may be a world that operates as a result of a network may be a world resource, whereas reserving an associate degree data processing address may be a regional operation as a result of the address may be a local resource.

As you begin to optimize your Google Cloud applications, it is vital to know these regions and zones act. As an example, notwithstanding you'll, you would not wish to connect a disk in one area to a PC during a different location due to the latency you'd introduce would create a poor performance. Thankfully, Google Cloud will not allow you to do that; disks will solely be hooked up to computers within the same zone.

Depending on the extent of self-management needed for the computing and hosting service you opt for, you may or may not have to be compelled to consider, however, and wherever resources area unit allotted.

WAYS TO ACT WITH THE SERVICES

Google Cloud provides you with three primary ways to act with the services and resources. The Google Cloud Console provides a web-based, graphical interface that you simply will use to manage your Google Cloud comes and resources. Once you use the Cloud Console, you produce a replacement project, opt for an associate degree existing project, and use the resources you simply make within that project's context. You'll be able to produce multiple; therefore, you'll be able to use comes to separate your add no matter approach is sensible for you. For example, you may begin a replacement project if you would like to create certain solely sure team members will access this project's resources. In contrast, all team members will still access resources in another project.

You can run Google cloud commands within the following ways:

You can install the Cloud SDK. The SDK includes the Google cloud tool. Therefore you'll be able to open a terminal window on your pc and run commands to manage Google Cloud resources.

You can use Cloud Shell, which may be browser-based. As a result of it runs during a browser window, you do not have to be compelled to install something on your PC. You'll be able to open the Cloud Shell from the Google Cloud Console.

- Cloud Shell provides the following:
- A temporary cipher Engine virtual machine instance.
- An intrinsical code editor.
- 5 GB of persistent disk storage.
- Pre-installed Cloud SDK and different tools.
- Language support for Java, Go, Python, Node.Js, PHP, Ruby, and NET.

WEB PREVIEW PRACTICALITY.

Built-in authorization for access to Cloud Console comes and resources.

For a listing of Google cloud commands, see the Google cloud reference.

For a lot of data regarding Cloud Shell, see How google Cloud Shell works.

CLIENT LIBRARIES

The Cloud SDK includes client libraries that change you to produce and manage resources simply. Google Cloud shopper libraries expose APIs for two primary purposes:

- App APIs provide access to services. App Apis area unit optimized for supported languages, like Node.js and Python. The libraries' area unit is designed around service metaphors; therefore, you'll be able to work with the services a lot of natural and write less boilerplate code. The libraries additionally offer helpers for authentication and authorization.

- Admin APIs offer practicality for resource management. As an example, you'll be able to use admin Apis if you would like to make your automatic tools.

- You can also use the Google API shopper libraries to access Apis for a product like Maps, Drive, and YouTube.

Pricing

To browse evaluation details for individual services, see the price list.

To estimate your total prices for running a particular work on Google Cloud, see the pricing calculator.

As seen and discussed in the earlier chapters of this work, the data processing system exhausted concrete data processing needs. It is clear out rightly clear that the data processing system means the system of interrelated techniques and means of collecting and processing the data needed to organize control of some systems.

Here not only was the importance of the data processing system outlined, but best methods on how you can make the best out of it were also as well in the list; the work in the earlier chapters explained the steps to the effective management of data and data especially when it comes to the processing part. Tools for processing were outlined, detailed steps on how to use the processor, and various other means thereupon took care of. The work also explained how to build and concretely bring the data processing system into life and operation. Means on how to achieve the est on this platform was as well enlisted and concretely explained.

For every piece of work under the earth, there is in existence hindrances that prevent the smooth running of such limitations were given long-lasting solutions in this work, some of these are as follows.

Codify the decision process. It is the core step in creating knowledge for all decision logic that transcend individuals and organizations; this means once documented, the decision logic can now be shared, improved, updated, audited, tested, and simulated

Record the decisions and factors and data that led to the decision. Here business decisions, interactions with costumers, or the way they are treated are governed y regulations and must remain compliant with legal or business best practices.

Modeling the analytics for making model decisions. Just creating a predictive analytic algorithm is not enough; being able to share best practices and create cross-organizational collaboration provides opportunities to efficiently scale the use of and the power of analytics throughout an Enterprise.

Optimizing the models as business conditions. Such optimizatio9n through the decision automation process provides two instincts and unique opportunities: a chance to fine-tune a decision for a better way to align with business priorities and, secondly, the ability to simulate changes modifications of such decision-making process.

Adaptation of models for applying multiple decision scenarios that can improve decision by measuring results, evaluating successes, and optimizing further this is what the machine learning and artificial intelligence are made up of.

This work has done a complete and concrete explanation of the necessary ICT basics, especially on Google cloud.

APPRECIATION

We sincerely appreciate your book's purchase that reveals useful data about everything you need to know about Google Professional Data Engineering. We hope you loved it.

Thanks,

Jason Hoffman.

GOOGLE PROFESSIONAL CLOUD ARCHITECT

Disclaimer

The content of this book has been checked and compiled with great care. For the completeness, correctness and topicality of the contents; however, no guarantee or guarantee can be taken over. This book's content represents the personal experience and opinion of the author and is for entertainment purposes only. The content should not be confused with medical help.

There will be no legal responsibility or liability for damages resulting from counterproductive exercise or errors by the reader. No guarantee can be given for success. The author, therefore, assumes no responsibility for the non-achievement of the goals described in the book.

CHAPTER ONE - GOOGLE CERTIFIED PROFESSIONAL ARCHITECT OVERVIEW

Introduction

Google certified professional Architecture is a program for individuals who have an interest in Google cloud computing architecture or cloud computing services. They must undergo the rigorous assessment of this program to have the certification needed and attain the name or become a Google cloud certified professional architect on Google cloud platform.

Individuals take up this program for boosting their careers, depending on their areas of interest. Google cloud platforms offer different certification programs or courses for individuals interested or Information Technology expertise. Programs such as:

1. **Professional Data Engineer:** This program enables the abilities in developing data engineering, building data collection, data processing including design and machine learning on Google cloud platform(GCP)

2. **Professional Cloud Developer:** This program promotes in delivering full-stack knowledge and skills in the scalable application of the Google cloud platform model.

3. **Professional Cloud Security Engineering:** This course is exclusively meant for future security engineers. They have the intention to secure the cloud infrastructure of the company using the Google cloud's platform security tools.

4. **Professional Cloud Architects:** This program helps in acquiring knowledge about complex cloud computing services in Google cloud platforms and are among the highest-paid professionals in the Google cloud platform profession.

5. **Professional Collaboration Engineers:** This is a course that is exclusively meant for individuals targeting to become a G-suite specialist in the later stage.

6. **Professional Cloud Network Engineer:** This program helps in designing, implementing and managing the architecture in the Google cloud platform model.

All of these and more are the numerous programs offered by Google as our world turn virtual by the day. All these certifications validate once expertise and show one's ability to transform businesses with Google cloud technology, but that's for that.

Google Certified Professional Architecture as a course, oversees the transfer of knowledge and understanding of cloud computing services, cloud computing architecture and its infrastructures. This certification program provides Google cloud professionals with a way to demonstrate their skills.

Google is an art or practice of designing and building of structures and components, even sub-components which are connected and deliver to an online platform. Elements that make-up clouds like hardware, virtual resources, management container, automation middleware and more are bound to create a cloud computing environment. So the integrating of the different technologies to create an information technology environment or cloud computing environment.

In cloud architecture, tools are required to create such, and these tools are known as **Cloud Infrastructure**. In an organization, Cloud architects are responsible for managing the cloud architecture, especially as cloud technologies grow increasingly complex. For a better understanding of what this Google cloud architecture is all about, and its components, the explanation of the reoccurring words or rather crucial words will be explained. Words like cloud, cloud computing services, cloud computing architecture and Google cloud platforms.

CLOUD

Cloud is a set of tools that help developers spend less time managing and more time creating.

What do I mean? Cloud are referred to as servers that are accessed over the internet, and the software and databases that run on those servers. Its also a platform that hosts several registering assets over the web as a helpful, on-request utility to be leased on a "pay-more only as costs arise premise". Clouds are virtualized data centres made up of computation and storage resources.

The case has not always been like this, however. It all started with what we call '**on-premise**' which is an installed software that runs on computers, on the premises of the person or organization that is using the software. Due to the fact it's within a limited environment, its server is limited too. For example, an organization has a computer with a single server and probably five users and the next day, there's a thousand user because a single server is being used it will crash. Then **scaling** came into play, which was seen to be a temporary remedy to on-premise. Scaling however involved the use of more than one computer, tons of coding and quite a bit of data sharing between the computers involved to link it. Scaling, therefore, helped to serve and reach more users than the on-premise software.

However, this scaling seems to be time and resource exhausting.

Then **time sharing** came about, which involved the sharing of computing resources among many users at the same time using multi-programming and multi-tasking.

With continued usage and passing of time, companies who owned and managed direct access to the sharing decided to add services like infrastructure as a Service(IaaS), Platform as a Service(PaaS), software as a Service(SaaS) which led to Cloud services as we know it today. Our daily lives are influenced by the Cloud system ranging from our emails, to apps used in shopping, to banking transactions, all of them use the cloud one way or another. Clouds have different models they offer based on diverse, unique business models. We have models such as;

- **Public cloud:** this is a cloud whose resources are shared by multiple customers. Each customer that procures the services of the cloud is known as a tenant. A public cloud can have numerous tenants sharing the same resources and services.

- **Private cloud:** here, the entire cloud is reserved for one occupant, and as an occupant, you can design the cloud according to your demand. You can also be connected to a private cloud by the use of either a private LAN or over the internet.

- **Hybrid cloud:** as the name implies, a hybrid cloud is a combination of public and private cloud, making the best of both worlds available. When the space on the hybrid cloud is exhausted and needs to be increased, extra resources are borrowed from the public cloud, and this occurrence is called cloud bursting. Hybrid cloud gives you room to host a few of your applications on a public cloud and other crucial ones on a private cloud. It provides you with cost and resource savings according to your needs.

Google cloud platform

Google cloud platform is a public cloud-based machine which delivers services to customers on as you go basis. This platform allows business businesses to rent the software services and servers of Google themselves, instead of paying very hefty sum on-premise local servers. One can use Google enterprise suite of services and their immense computing power.

Cloud Computing Service

The term cloud computing service includes the activities that are carried out over the cloud. It is the optimization of services such as storage, applications, and servers over the cloud platform.

Most organizations go to cloud services to reduce their investment in support costs, framework costs, and guaranteeing the accessibility of assets nonstop, cloud computing is, therefore, a more efficient and cost-effective solution than traditional data centres. With all these, we see how efficient cloud computing service is, and this is due to its architectural framework, which is cloud computing architecture.

Cloud Computing Architecture

Cloud Computing architecture can be said to be as the different components and subcomponents that have been designed in terms of application, software capacities, databases, and so many more to maximize the function of cloud resources in other to provide long-lasting business solutions. Cloud Computing architecture is made up of three fundamental components, which include; Front-end platform, Back-end platform and cloud-based delivery.

Front-end Platform: front-end platform infrastructure includes everything that the end-user can interact with; it is a broader collection of different sub-components that together offer the user interface. The Front-end cloud architecture forms an essential part of how end-users connect to cloud computing architecture. This Front-end architecture includes components like; local network, web applications and web browsers. Specific components comprise the main front-end cloud architecture. Components such as;

User interface: this component refers to all of the elements that the end-user accesses to send request or perform any task on the cloud. Some of the popular cloud-based user interfaces include; g-mail and Google documents

Client system or network: this is a critical part of the front end cloud architecture. This client system or network refers to the hardware at the end-users end. It could be a PC or any input device. When it comes to Google computing architecture, the client-side system doesn't require extraordinary abilities to process the heavy load. The cloud can store the entire massive data and also process it.

The Software

This is a significant component in the front end architecture that operates and works on the user's experience. The software component in the front-end architecture makes up the client-end applications or browsers.

Back-end

On the other hand, the back end is the "cloud" part of computing architecture, comprising all the resources required to deliver cloud-computing services. A systems back end can be made up of several bare metal servers, data storage facilities, virtual machines, a security mechanism and services, all built-in conformance with a deployment model, and altogether responsible for providing a service. The back end architecture must align with the front-end. Comprises of the storage and hardware components, which are found on a remote server. The cloud service provider oversees and manages the cloud platform from the back-end. Ordinarily, the back-end cloud architecture should be strong and durable because it holds the entire infrastructure on the cloud.

The prime of the back-end cloud architecture are:

Storage: the data of a cloud application reside in cloud storage. Several cloud service providers offer different data storage; one thing they have in common is a reserved section for cloud storage. Example of storages are; hard-drives, solid-state drive etc. The storage in the cloud is formed by the hard drives in the server bays, back-end architecture and especially in the framework of cloud computing, the product parcels, the drives according to the requirements of the OS in the cloud to run multiple services.

Application: This application is a substantial element of the back-end architecture. It requires the user interface that the back-end platform provides the end-users with, to send queries. This part of the back-end takes care of the clients' request and requirements.

Infrastructure: this refers to the systems that direct all the cloud software services. This workload will always determine the infrastructure model. It includes; central processing unit(CPU), motherboard, graphics processing unit(GPU), accelerator cards, etc.

Management: In technical terms specific resources to specific tasks and responsibilities for the flawless functioning of any cloud environment is allocated by the management software, management is the 'middleware', and it coordinates between the front-end and back-end architecture in a cloud computing system.

Security: An integral and crucial part of cloud computing infrastructure is security. Security infrastructure is created by keeping the debugging in mind. Debugging should be easy, in case of any issue. Regular storage is the first thing to do to make security guaranteed. After which, you can affect virtual firewalls and other necessary elements that are critical in cloud security design or architecture.

Internet:

The medium through which the front end and the back end platforms interacts and communicate with each other is the internet.

Service: this is the essential aspect of the back-end cloud architecture through which the whole back-end cloud architecture receives utility from. Its function is to manage every task that is operated on the cloud computing architecture, which includes some cloud services such as web services, storage and app development environment. It is important also to mention that service can carry out a vast range of functions on the cloud run-time.

Cloud-based Delivery

Cloud-based delivery is any form of operation that a provider can offer through infrastructure, software and platforms. Therefore, if your business used Google Drive or Office 365, then you are making use of cloud-based delivery. In addition, other cloud-based delivery subscription-like "Platform-as-a-Service(PaaS)", and "Infrastructure-as-a-service(IaaS)", etc, are made possible.

Their subscriptions just have a few difference as an individual or organization can purchase to make use of the software that is commonly referred to as Software-as-a-Service(SaaS), all thanks to technological innovations like virtualization and hypervisors.

You should know that Cloud-based delivery can dine both privately and publicly through the internet. It can be retained within an organizations network when used over an intranet, and it is possible to combine both.

Software as a Service(SaaS)

This cloud computing administration is additionally alluded to as cloud application service; the model of delivery includes the provision of cloud computing services through authorized software or subscription.

The end-users don't need to purchase or install any hardware for this cloud-based delivery model in their respective location, and this is because in most case, SaaS applications operate directly through the web browser, consequently eliminating any requirement to download or install the applications.

Some common examples of SaaS are:

- Cisco WebEx
- Google Apps
- Slack
- HubSpot
- Salesforce Dropbox

Platform as a Service(PaaS)

"Platform as a service" is also referred to as cloud platform service, in a way, it has similarities with the SaaS. The point of divergence, however, is that PaaS offers a platform for the creation of software. SaaS, on the other hand, gives unrestricted access to software through the internet without any platform need or demand.

The essence of "PaaS" being a cloud-based delivery model, is to provide the opportunity to operate, create, and also manage apps on the cloud computing architecture for the end-users. In this delivery pattern, the hardware and software components are organized by a third-party service provider

Examples of "Paas" are:

- Force.com
- Windows Azure
- Magneto Commerce Cloud
- OpenShift

Infrastructure as a Service(IaaS)

It can also be referred to as cloud infrastructure services; this cloud-based delivery model supports computer hardware such as data centre space, storage, and networking technology as a service. It further helps to deliver virtualization technology and operation

system—Infrastructure's responsibility as a Service is to manage middleware, application data and run-time environments.

Examples of Infrastructure as a Service includes:

- Amazon Web Services (AWS) EC2
- Google Compute Engine (GCE)
- Cisco Metapod

Having seen the components of google cloud architecture and how it functions and delivers services to the end-users we know look the essence of google cloud computing architecture;

Cost-Effectiveness

This being one of the important reasons why you should make use of cloud computing architecture, and it is because no physical hardware investments are required in cloud computing, this consequently, helps you to save significant capital costs.

Besides, you do not need to hire trained personnel for the hardware maintenance; the cloud service provider deals with the purchasing and maintenance of your equipment.

Access to the Latest Technology

Another importance cloud computing architecture is that it gives you a competitive edge and advantage over your competition, making the most recent and modern tech applications available at your fingertips. Which consequently reduces the money and time that would have been spent on installation processes.

Faster Connectivity

You are empowered to deploy, your service in lesser chicks quickly with cloud computing. The ripple effect of deploying quicker can access the necessary resources for your system within no time.

Data Backup and Restoration

When data is stored in a cloud storage architecture, it is relatively easier to backup and recovers any lost information without hassles; this helps to save time that would have otherwise be spent on time taking process.

Reliability

This informs why many subscribe to cloud computing services. One can rely on cloud computing architecture for an instant update about any modification or changes.

Remoteness

One can desire to work remotely from their home, and if you want to, cloud computing architecture is your primary precedence. It is because it allows employees who are working at remote locations to access all they need on cloud services easily. Mobility is guaranteed if there is internet connectivity.

Scalability and Flexibility

The cloud computing architecture is appropriate for businesses that have a growth or fluctuation bandwidth demand making it very easy for businesses to scale up their cloud capacity and experience by merely modifying their usage plan, and if the business chooses to scale down the cloud-based service provider can also make that possible, on the flip side, the level of **flexibility** that cloud computing architecture provides for businesses would give it a competitive edge over other competitors.

IT Readiness

Cloud computing architecture is known to influence brands to embrace the IT age more swiftly. It is quite vital since almost everyone uses smartphones. Businesses are therefore enabled to better communicate with their customers or even internal staffs on any platform at all, by embracing the cloud, and this consequently results in an increased capacity to produce a more customized experience.

In all, it has become pronounced that architecture or cloud computing provides a great advantage for businesses. The adoption and implementation of Google cloud architecture give businesses a higher competitive edge in terms of increased productivity and lower cost.

Therefore, it is of importance for an ambitious organization that seek to succeed in the Post-IT age to leverage on the opportunities abundant in cloud computing architecture. So it is time to overlook the on-premise hosting and become very accessible through the most recent IT that are available on the cloud.

We have recent IT clouds like; Amazon web services, Google cloud platform, etc., whose infrastructure have been placed to meet peoples need or organization demands.

Google cloud platform let's organization take advantage of the robust network and cloud computing architecture or the technologies that Google uses to deliver its products. Global companies like Coca-Cola and cutting edge technology stars like Spotify are already running sophisticated applications on the google cloud platform.

Putting all these together, we see how professional architecture as a course and its knowledge and application helps organizations in managing and providing cloud solutions infrastructure.

CHAPTER TWO - ARCHITECTING WITH GOOGLE COMPUTER ENGINE

In learning or getting ready to architect with the Google computer engine, a lot of things should be known and clearly understood.

Firstly, you should understand what a Google Computer Engine does in Google Cloud Architecture. The Google Computer Engine allows you to create and run virtual machines on Google Infrastructure. The computer engine offers a lot of things, including scale performance and value that would enable you to launch or start-up large computer clusters on Google's infrastructure. It has it also has its advantages that would allow you to run thousands of virtual CPU's on a system if the system has been originally designed to be fast and to give optimum consistency of performance, there are also no upfront investments. Google is preferably one of the best organizations as it is very efficient and plays out its role effectively. The Google Cloud Platform also supplies the Google Computer engine for infrastructure as in some service use cases like the IaaS. The Google Computer Engine also provides a very efficient computing infrastructure that allows us to select and consider the platform components that we will require. While working with the Google Computer Engine, we are required to administer, configure and carefully and expertly monitor the applications. It is our responsibility to handle provision and manage the systems. At the same time, Google makes sure that the resources needed are available, reliable and ready for us to use them. One advantage attached to this is the fact that we now have absolute control of our systems, and we can also enjoy unlimited flexibility. The Google Computer Engine offers different kinds of machine types to suit your requirements and specifications configuration and also to meet your budget and needs, where you can also decide which operating systems, programming languages, frameworks, services, tech or development stacks you prefer.

The Google Cloud Platform is just Google's public cloud offering, and it can be compared to some web services like the Microsoft Azure and the Amazon web services. But unlike the other web services, the Google Cloud Platform is built and created upon the Google's vast and massive, cutting edge infrastructure that takes care of the traffic and workload of all the Google users.

Next, we have to get ourselves conversant with who a cloud architect is and what a cloud architect does and also the kind of skills he requires. A Cloud Architect is an IT professional whose work it is to oversee the cloud computing strategy for a company, and it includes a few things like the cloud adoption plans, cloud management and monitoring and the cloud application design. The cloud architect has to inspect and oversee the application architecture and the deployment in cloud environments, including the public cloud, the private cloud and the hybrid cloud. The cloud architects also have to stay informed and updated as they also act as consultants to their organizations on the latest trends, issues and information. Also, a Google Cloud architect must possess the following skills, or you must be able to do the following:

You must have the skill of programming languages: even while concentrating on the Google Cloud platform, knowing and understanding other programming languages like java, python, pearl etc. will improve and cover your bases for the cloud infrastructure and some cloud-native apps like the Kubernetes is also written in Go programming language.

Also, you must possess the multi-cloud architecture skill because the most convenient ways for organizations and enterprises to migrate their clouds most times if they follow the rules of privacy regulations is through the multi and hybrid strategies. Although it is advised to stick to one strategy on cloud suite, it is also detrimental as those who tend to have acquisitions can wind up with a multi-cloud strategy by default.

An almost ordinary and most essential skill a Cloud architect must-have is the Data storage skill, this includes the knowledge and information of infrastructure and hardware specifically for those who will be handling jobs with on-prem clouds, storage buckets, provisioning, capacity planning and of course data security. Also, you must possess content presentation and communication skills as they are essential and essential as it is known that cloud architects are often told to explain their work to their non-technical colleagues

Another skill to be possessed or acquired by a cloud architect is that of teamwork as leading a team is often expected of cloud architects. You should be able to manage people, handle ideas professionally and expertly and also solve problems.

Cloud architects must also learn how to change with the cloud, and the skill sets needed to work with it. They must be flexible to new technologies and must also have the attitude to pick them quickly and master them skillfully. So one that aspires to be a Google Cloud Architect and wants to begin or get started on building architectural diagrams of the Google Cloud Platform. You must learn, clear out and understand the following things which will help you fully understand how to develop or create a step by step diagram that runs and applies on the Google Cloud Platform we will be using a platform known as the Lucidchart.

Now we must understand the basics of the Lucidchart because this is one of the primary aspects of becoming a cloud architect. The Lucidchart is a web-based commercial or business service that allows users to join ideas, collaborate and work together in real-time to create flowcharts, UML designs, software prototypes, mind maps and organizational charts and many other diagram types. With the Lucidchart, you are allowed and free to share your dynamic ideas in the form of diagrams to the world. The Lucidchart is built on many web standards like the JavaScript and HTML5 and is also supported and allowed in many common web browsers like the Mozilla Firefox, the Google Chrome, Microsoft Edge, Safari and Internet Explorer. The Lucidchart platform has been recommended to users by Google as an ideal platform for building diagrams.

The Lucidchart has an online diagramming app that aids and assists real-time collaborative editing, to make it easy to draw it provides online diagramming and create flowcharts, org charts, wireframes UML, and more; it gives up many options for exporting and presenting your diagrams and is also equipped with well-stocked libraries of objects and templates too. This online diagramming app of the Lucidchart has its advantages and disadvantages. The benefits of the online diagramming app Lucidchart are it is very responsive, it is also easy to learn; it offers excellent collaboration and also provides the smooth user experience, the web app also works efficiently when offline and it also integrates with many other apps and services. It integrates with G Suite, Google Drive, Microsoft Office, Slack and more, and it imports Visio, OmniGirrafe to draw files, it runs on all major browsers. It is also stocked with shape libraries for many scenario's; like the flowcharts and process maps, Azure, AWS and GCP shapes, mockups and wireframes, UML, ER, and network diagrams, mind maps and Venn diagrams, org charts and BPMN diagrams. Then for its intuitive features, it has links and layers for interactive pictures, drag and drops functionality, auto prompt for quickly adding and connecting objects, interactive mockups with hotspots and current and future states, monitor processes, systems and goals through linking data and conditional formatting. It is also perfect for teams; like in the real-time collaboration, in editor group chat and comments, version control and revision history, build and share customized templates and make custom shape libraries. For the disadvantages, it doesn't allow desktop apps and also it is difficult to access its pricing and plan options.

Unlike some people who are not designers but require diagrams for some compelling presentations software like the flowchart and diagramming software will be needed for cases like that. The Lucidchart is just one of the best because it is a web app that can work on all computers that has a web browser and possesses an offline mode to keep you productive even when you aren't connected to the internet. With this web app, it is easy to create and publish diagrams that look professional. One close competitor with the Lucidchart is the SmartDraw which is also an editors' choice. Still, it doesn't have a productive offline work mode like the Lucidchart but then it comes with a much bigger library and collection of objects and templates. The Lucidchart offers a few ranks of service. It provides a free personal account that can be used until infinity. Still, it offers limited storage and templates and only gives access to a library with basic shapes for creating diagrams and flowcharts. If you wish to be granted access to more features and storage on this tier of the Lucidchart plan you'd have to pay for an upgrade as the in-app prices may be altered depending on the kind of selections you make during signup, it might be a monthly or an annual plan.

The Lucidchart has been improved, and its latest version has a few changes and upgrades. The newest version of the Lucidchart has integrations with the capacity and ability to take in or instead pull in and use data from elsewhere in your diagrams. Still, for this feature to be accessed, it must be paid for, you can now connect and get data imported from apps like Confluence, GitHub, JIRA, Slack, Salesforce and a lot of other apps. The main aim of these integrations is to make or create live diagrams that update in real-time and even possess more value beyond being illustrative.

How To Get Started With The Lucid Chart:

Firstly you need to signup, now the signup procedure is a simple one and doesn't require or disturb for a credit card. You can just easily put in your email address and create a password, or you can just sign up using Google or Office 365 account for validation, this is also the same with starting a new document, and it is straightforward whether you decide to use of the templates from the Lucidchart or you decide to make use of a blank document. For a blank document, you would know how to work your way around some shapes and text boxes because of its freehand, but if you decide to use a template, there are already a selection of squares, basic rectangles, text boxes and arrows on the page. If you check out the left bar, you'll notice that more shapes are made available. It is also straightforward to learn how to move the shapes around; duplicate them group them and ungroup them, rotate and resize them and a lot more. The user experience in the Lucidchart is more natural than in some other online diagramming apps, it is fast and responsive and figuring how to use it takes no stress or little brainpower when it comes to any diagramming app like the Lucidchart the selection of templates can either build or mar the diagramming app. When creating flowcharts, network infrastructure diagrams, floor plans and complicated designs templates and libraries are required as their absence in the diagramming work can and will leave a non-designer confused and unsure of what next to do or the next action to take. It is this aspect of diagramming that differentiates the diagramming software from the more general-purpose vector and graphics applications like for example the Adobe Illustrator. The primary selections of the Lucidchart are fully illustrated, most notably at the pro level. And this is because most of the very best software has an extensive and broad selection of shapes and templates for a crowd of uses. Even as good as the Lucidchart is and also as plentiful as its template and shapes selection is abundant, the SmartDraw's shapes and templates collection is much bigger and vast, and it also covers a lot of grounds that the Lucidchart doesn't cover at all. In the SmartDraw, you'll be able to find available templates and shapes for world maps, crime scenes, emergency evacuations and anatomy too. The Lucidchart doesn't possess all these templates because its selection isn't all that expansive and broad, so for diagrams that will require these listed specifications, the SmartDraw app should be used to work it out. Also, another necessary part of the diagramming software is how it aids to display your complete work or finished product. Using the Lucidchart diagrams can be exported to JPEG, PDF, SVG and PNG with transparent backgrounds and some others too. An option is also included on whether to export the CSV shape of your data. A team of one or many which of the two you work, some times will present themselves, such times as when you need to share your work with others. It could be that you need to communicate an essential and complicated process to a client, or peradventure you want to collaborate on new project information from others. The Lucidchart proffers sharing solutions and options that make it less difficult to collaborate in real-time, process and gather feedback from others directly in the Lucidchart and also to change permission levels as the project evolves. And just because the Lucidchart is cloud-based and also available on all devices and browsers, there is certainly no barrier to working with others. Also, the Lucidchart is always up to date, and current on the latest developments or changes, and no one has to install expensive software on their computer or devices.

Now to understand the aspect of the collaboration tools in the Lucidchart, the Lucidchart has the capability and ability to collaborate with others at all account levels. We must also see that the Lucidchart was built for better collaboration from the origin or the beginning. However, there are still limitations of the account that still apply during the collaboration. A good instance is this one; when a person with a Team subscription invites a free account holder to collaborate on a diagram, now the file can only be edited by the free user if it has or possess fewer than 60 objects on it and also if it doesn't include any purposes that are limited to the paid accounts. A whole lot of diagramming apps aid and support collaboration, some of these diagramming apps is SmartDraw, Creately, and Visio. The competence of these apps to collaborate in real-time is soon becoming a standard feature in diagramming apps, most notably the cloud-based apps. On the invitation of another Lucidchart user or member to collaborate, you can make decisions of if they can edit, edit and share, comment only or view only. In the Team and Enterprise accounts, the admins can include limits to the sharing permissions in such a way that it allows sharing only to other users within the organization. Collaboration performs much the same way as it usually does in Google Documents and some other G Suite apps, like Sheets and Slides. When more than one individual has a file open, people can see who is in the document and the changes made as they work. Collaborators also have a chatbox for a live discussion of issues, and also a provision for commenting tools for asynchronous communication. Like I said earlier, the Lucidchart is very easy to learn and is adequately stocked with objects and templates and is an excellent choice for diagramming software. It provides exceptional and adequate collaboration support amongst team members. It is reasonably priced even though it also has some tremendous value-adding features, though it might be a little difficult selecting the plan that will work best for you and what you plan to do

CHAPTER THREE - PREPARATION FOR THE PROFESSIONAL CLOUD ARCHITECT EXAM

To ace this exam, you must prepare very well and study wide to acquire more information on the course. You must obtain specific skills to get more conversant with the questions that would be asked on the exam day. You must also learn to follow laid down rules as breaching of any of the rules will cost you some precious points in the exam.

Here are some tips and ideas on how you can prepare for the professional cloud architect exam and be confident about acing the test below:

1. **UNDERSTAND THE CONCEPTS OF THE HYBRID CLOUD.**

   To understand this subheading, you must first understand that a hybrid cloud is a combination of a private cloud joined with the use of public cloud services where one or more connection points exist between the environments. The main aim and objective are to combine services and data from a variety of cloud models to develop a unified automated and properly managed computing environment. The hybrid cloud services are compelling because it is known to combine the two cloud services to give businesses and firms more significant control over their private data. An example of the hybrid cloud is the AWS the Amazon Web Services with composition among the various platforms. It also enables convenient, on-demand network access to a shared source of configurable computing resources that can be quickly provisioned and released to the sources with little or no management effort or service provider interaction.

You must understand that there is a great deal of prominence on the connecting on-premises infrastructure to the Google Cloud Platform. You must clearly understand the picture and be able to make necessary connections on how to make the right chain. You must always understand completely the choices/ decisions and improvements that necessitate the corresponding loss of increasing in extent an enterprise data centre to the Google Cloud Platform.

Just like its other competitors, Google has a good number of channels to connect devices installed to be used only on the premises to the cloud. Every channel has its own specific and unique attribute that handles and takes care of a particular enterprise outline of an expected or supposed sequence of events. You must also be careful to understand the rules; the dos and don'ts of using one service against the other while trying to carry out the hybrid strategy. You must learn to mind and give attention to hybrid networking services offered by Google. The cloud VPN safely connects installed devices on the premises to the Google Cloud Platform VCP through the public internet. It is also cheap and safe, which slightly differs from the Cloud Interconnect, which delivers unmatched connectivity but is quite expensive. The direct peering is also a less expensive choice to the Cloud Interconnect that provides better performance than a VPN. It doesn't have an SLA, but it sure allows customers a direct connection to Google by a significant reduction on the fees.

2. KNOW HOW TO MOVE DATA TO GOOGLE CLOUD

Another essential and necessary step in migration is moving data to the Google cloud. A suitable technique is the online data transfer which is capable of moving large amounts of existing backup images and archived documents and files to extremely low cost and highly available storage provided through the Google's Nearline and Coldline storage classes. Google offers multiple services for moving data to Google Cloud Platform.

To carry out basic operations on the Google Cloud Storage, you must become conversant with the command-line tool. You must understand how to equally distance uploads, set up security and enhance the data migration with gsutil. The gsutil comes in handy to migrate a large number of files from local storage to the cloud.

The cloud storage transfer has become an ideal choice to move large amounts of data from other cloud platforms. The Transfer appliance is one of the best options when terabytes or petabytes of data need to be transferred to the Google Cloud Platform. It is also designed to reduce lengthy transfer times, making it faster, and it reduces risks that come with moving data over the internet to the public cloud. To use this Transfer appliance a customer requests for it from Google, and it is shipped into the customer's location. The customer's data is moved to the device and sent backed to Google, who now uploads it to the Google Cloud Storage service. After this process is done, the device is wiped by Google to ensure security measures and prevent underlying risks if the customer intends to migrate large datasets (a large file of related records on a computer medium) directly to the BigQuery Data Transfer Service, which automates data migration from SaaS applications to Google BigQuery on a planned, arranged and orderly basis.

To gain more understanding of this, we would research more into the usefulness of the BigQuery Data Transfer Service. The BigQuery Data Transfer Service is a Serverless, highly scalable, and cost-effective multi-cloud warehouse designed and programmed for business agility, speed and reliance. The BigQuery Data runs analytics at a scale of 26%-34% lower than three years TCO than cloud data warehouse alternatives, it aids to predict business outcomes and results with built-in machine learning and without the need to migrate data. It also aids customers to easily create comprehensive reports and dashboards using popular business intelligence tools, outside the normal and also assists to securely access and share analytical insights or ideas in your organization with a few clicks.

Here are some key features of the BigQuery

I) BigQuery Omni (private alpha)

It is a tractable, multi-cloud analytics solution, powered by Anthos that allows the user access to analyze data across clouds using standard SQL and BigQuery's familiar interface to answer questions and share results from your device across your datasets.

II) BigQuery ML

The BigQuery ML enables data scientists and data analysts to build and test out ML models on semi-structured data straight into the BigQuery, using simple SQL in a very small amount of time.

III) BigQuery BI Engine

The BigQuery BI Engine is an exceedingly fast-in-memory analysis service for BigQuery that allows customers and users to analyze or process large and complex datasets fairly with sub-second query response time and high concurrency. The Engine integrates with known tools which will help to accelerate data exploration and analysis.

3. LEARN GOOGLE CLOUD IAM IN DETAIL

The Google Cloud IAM (Identity and Access Management) allows administrators to give power to who can go to work on specific essential resources allowing the user maximum control and authority to manage Google Cloud resources centrally. The Google Cloud IAM gives up a central view into security policy across your entire enterprise for organizations and businesses with composite and complicated organizational structures and workgroups to reduce compliance processes. Due to the knowledge of the fact that a business's internal structure and policies can get composite fast and can also change dynamically, the Cloud IAM is specially designed to help simplify a lot of the complex changes. It is designed with a decent universal interface that lets the user manage access control across all Google Cloud resources consistently. Once this is known, it can be applied in any place.

Due to the inevitable fact that Permissions Control can be a time-consuming process, the program "Recommender" is written to aid admins in removing unwanted access to Google Cloud resources by the machine learning how to make smart access control recommendations. With this program, Recommender can easily detect or notice overly permissive access and put them in the correct order based on the same type of users in the enterprise and their access patterns. The Google Cloud IAM also makes the provision of tools to handle resource permissions with little or no complains and high automation. The users are granted access only to the specific tools needed to get their job done and completed, and the admins can easily grant permissions by default to an entire group of users. It also allows users to give access to cloud resources at the minimum level access well beyond the project level access. It creates more minute access control policies to resources based on attributes like IP address, resource type and more. These laid down guidelines ensure that accurate security controls are in a position when granting access to Google Cloud Resources. The Google Cloud IAM also lets you pay attention to business policies around your resources and makes carrying out instructions easy. It also has an in-built audit trail for the admins to get information on the history of permissions removal and delegation. Google Cloud also makes business and organizations identification easy. The Google Leverage Cloud Identity is an inbuilt managed identity created to harmonize the user's accounts over apps and projects efficiently. The Google Admin Console makes it very easy to set up single sign-on and configure two-factor authentication. You're also granted access to the Google Cloud Organization which allows and gives you the user to manage projects through the Resource Manager mainly.

Some features of the Google Cloud IAM are listed below:

1) No additional costs:

The Google Cloud IAM offers services for no extra or additional charges for all the cloud customers. You would only be charged for the use of the other Google Cloud services. Both the access to the Google Cloud IAM is free of charge.

II) Supple Roles:

Previously before the Google Cloud IAMthe, only persons with access to users were the Owner, the editor and the viewer. So a large variety of services and resources now present additional Google Cloud IAM roles out of the box.

III) Single and simple access control interface:

The Google Cloud IAM gives up a non-complex and straightforward stable access control interface for all the Google Cloud services.

IV) An in-built audit trail

An in-built audit trail is made available and accessible to the admins to ease compliance procedures for your organization.

You must also comprehend the key differences between the user accounts and the service accounts. You must see that the real users use the user accounts while the service accounts are used by the system services such as databases, web servers, and mail transport agents. The service accounts are also a lot like the IAM (Identity and Access Management) roles for EC2 where instances try to take over the meaning of a part. A service account is needed to connect the Compute engine VMs to the Google Cloud SQL instances. You must also see and understand how permissions propagate within the IAM hierarchy. You must also understand the four levels involved in setting IAM policies hierarchically; Organizational level, Folder level, Project level, Resource level.

The Organizational level:

The organization resource stands in for your company or enterprise. The IAM roles allowed at this level of the hierarchy are all gained or inherited by all resources under the organization.

The Folder level:

The folders can occupy or carry projects, other folders or even a combination of both. The roles allowed at the highest folder level will be obtained accordingly by other folders that are contained in the parent folder.

The Project level:

The projects stand-in for the trust limit or boundary among your company services, among the same project has a default level of trust. Resources inherit identity and Access Management roles, given access at the project level within that particular project.

The Resource level:

Resources like Genomics data sets, Subtopics, and Compute Engine Instances aid in support of lower-level roles to enable you as a user permit certain other users to a single resource within a project just like the existing Cloud Storage and BigQuery ACL systems.

IAM policies are hierarchical and progress down the structure. The union of the policy is the active policy and the policy inherited from its parent.

You must also learn how to reflect your Google resource hierarchy structure into your organizational structure. It must reflect the structure of your company's organization or arrangement, whether it's a start-up, SME, or a large corporation. An organization resource is advised for larger companies with more departments and teams where each team is in charge and control of their own set of applications and services. However, a start-up might first play out with a flat resource hierarchy with no organization resource. You must also set policies at the project level organization level instead of the setting them at the resource level because as new resources are included, you might want them to inherit their policies from their parent resource automatically. Just like when new virtual machines are involved in the project through auto-scaling, they immediately and automatically inherit the policy on the project, you should also learn to use projects to group resources that share the same boundary. Just like resources for the same products can belong to or be owned by the same project. Also make sure to use labels to add metadata to a document, group, and filter resources. You must always make sure to remember that the policies obtained by the child resources where gotten from the parent resources. And you must learn to grant roles at the minimum scope needed, just like when a user needs access to publish messages to a Pub/Subtopic he has to be granted the publisher's role to handle that topic. The Pub/Sub topics and subscriptions are resources that live under a project. If you would also like to limit project creation in your organization, the access organization policy must be changed to allow the Project Creator role to a group managed by you.

The Google Cloud Storage supports both the IAM and ACL policies. IAM is preferable when you want to protect buckets while the ACL's are great for safeguarding individual objects stored in buckets. You must understand their effective policies when they are both active.

4. SELECT THE APPROPRIATE CLOUD STORAGE AND DATABASE OFFERINGS

Unlike its competitors, the Google Cloud Platform has extraordinary and unique storage tiers that can deliver more value and services to the customers at a lower price, just the same way it is with the Google Cloud Platform database and broad data offerings.

When selecting the appropriate cloud storage; there are things you need to put into consideration:

I. You must consider the security capabilities as it is one of the most important factors restricting business holders from embracing the cloud. Involving the use of a storage Cloud provider is more like handing over private information to a third party and a third eye with the hopes of safeguarding it. So in the process of selecting a Cloud Storage provider, one must ensure that all-sufficient security measures are taken. These include anti-virus software, data encryption, firewalls and routine security checkups.

II. You must also consider the data storage location; storing data in the cloud involves storing it in an actual physical location, just transferred over the internet. When it comes to storing Cloud data you must understand your Cloud data location as storing data in a different country might attract a few issues, just like a change of laws in the country can affect who has access to the Cloud data. You should also consider the location if it is at risk for natural disasters like earthquakes, tsunamis, hurricanes and tornadoes. You should know your Cloud vendor plan in case of an emergency because it can play a significant role in protecting and saving your data.

III. Another thing to consider is price. There are so many Cloud vendors striving for your business, so the prices have become very competitive. A lot of providers offer a particular amount of storage for free, but businesses that require a lot more storage will need to pay for their services. You should understand how the vendors charge their clients and work out the best pricing plan that is suitable for your company.

IV. The service level agreement should be a significant factor to be taken into consideration when deciding a cloud storage provider. The service level agreement primarily highlights the work of a vendor for your company and the responsibility of the client. The items included are about the kind of data to be stored, how it will be stored and protected, how the problems will be solved and a lot more. Make sure you understand the prospective cloud vendor's service level agreement entails.

V. The last, however, not the least thing to consider is tech support, and this is because problems will always arise at different occasions. But you must also understand that the cloud provider can be contacted for assistance, so while you choose a vendor to ensure to ask them how they handle each support, you should also find out from them their available days and note how quickly they respond to problems. You must observe all these essential factors in a vendor to avoid the ones who do not meet up with your required needs.

Also, you must take note of when to use regional, multi-regional, nearline and coldline storage tiers when uploading and storing data in object storage. A nearline is used for when data is accessed at least once a month, and the coldline makes sense when the information is accessed only once a year.

The architects will be required to choose among a lot of different databases depending on their uses. You must also get used to the core and most essential aspects of the database, Cloud SQL, Cloud Spanner, Cloud Big table and BigQuery. The Cloud SQL gives up compatibility with already present MySQL and PostgreSQL databases. The BigQuery is meant for the storage and retrieving of large datasets with aid and support for ANSI SQL. And no, it is not a replacement to a NoSQL and RDBMS database server. The Cloud Dataflow is useful when data pipelines are to be built for streaming and batch processing scenarios.

CHAPTER FOUR - GETTING STARTED WITH GOOGLE KUBERNETES ENGINE

Kubernetes is an open-source container platform that removes so many of the manual processes involved in unfolding, scaling and managing containerized applications.

Google originally designed Kubernetes, and it is maintained by the Cloud Native Computing Foundation currently. Kubernetes aims to make available a "platform for automating scaling, deployment, furthermore, activities of utilization holders across groups of hosts", it works with a scope of compartment tools, which includes Docker.

Kubernetes can be seen as a stage offering support on many cloud administrations which offer a Kubernetes-based stage or framework as assistance (PaaS or IaaS). Many companies also provide their own branded Kubernetes distributions.

Made by similar designers that assembled Kubernetes, Google Kubernetes Engine (GKE) is a simple to utilize cloud-based Kubernetes administration for running containerized applications. GKE can assist you in executing an effective Kubernetes system for your applications in the cloud. With Anthos, Google offers a reliable Kubernetes experience for your applications across on-premises and different mists. Utilizing Anthos, you get a reliable, proficient, and confided in approach to run Kubernetes groups, anyplace.

Brief History About Kubernetes

he Greek word for Kubernetes is`κυβερνήτης`, meaning "helmsman" or "pilot." and the Tetymological root of cybernetics was founded by Joe Beda, Brendan Burns, and Craig McLuckie, first announced by Google in mid-2014 who was quickly joined by other Google engineers including Brian Grant and Tim Hockin. Google's Borg system heavily influences its development and design, which includes several high ranking contributors to the project previously worked on Borg. The initial codename for Kubernetes within Google was Project 7, a reference to the Star Trek ex-Borg character Seven of Nine. The seven spokes on the Kubernetes logo wheel referred that codename. However, the initial Borg project was written entirely in C++[10], but the rewritten Kubernetes system was implemented in Go.

July 21, 2015, was when Kubernetes v1.0 was released. Alongside with the Kubernetes v1.0 release, Google partnered with the Linux Foundation to form the Cloud Native Computing Foundation (CNCF) and gave Kubernetes as a seed technology. On March 6, 2018, Kubernetes Project reached the ninth place in submits at GitHub and second place in creators and issues to the Linux portion.

Features Of Kubernetes Google Engine

KUBERNETE PODS

A pod can be defined as a higher level of abstraction grouping containerized components. A pod consists of more than one containers that are guaranteed to be co-located on the host machine and can share resources. A pod is the basic scheduling unit in Kubernetes.

There's a unique Pod IP address that is assigned each pod in Kubernetes that is within the cluster, allowing applications to make use ports without any risk of conflict. All containers within the pod, can reference each other on local-host, but it has to use it Pod IP Address as a container within one pod has no means to address another container within another pod directly; for that, An application developer should never try to utilize the Pod IP Address, however, to reference/summon a capacity in another case, as Pod IP addresses are impermanent, on restart the particular case that they are referring to might be allocated to another Pod IP address. They should Instead use a Service reference, which also is referenced at the specific Pod IP Address to the target pod.

A pod can define a volume, like a network disk or local disk directory a, and then exposing it to the containers in the pod. Pods can be manually managed via the Kubernetes API or can be delegated to a controller by their management. Volumes such as this are also the basis for the Kubernetes features of Configure Maps (access to the configuration is provided through the filesystem apparent to the holder) and Secrets (to give admittance to certifications expected to get to distant assets safely, by delivering those credentials on the filesystem visible only to authorized containers).

CLUSTERORCHESTRATIONWITH GKE

The Kubernetes open-source cluster management system powers GKE clusters, Kubernetes provides the mechanisms and platforms through which you better or properly interact with your cluster. Kubernetes commands and resources are used to test and manage your applications, set policies, perform administration tasks, and help monitor the health of workloads you have deployed.

Kubernetes leverages on the similar design principles that run the popular Google services, and it provides some benefits: liveness probes for application containers automatic management, monitoring and, rolling updates, automatic scaling, and more likes. You're using technology based on Google's 10+ years of experience running production workloads in containers when you run your applications on a cluster.

KUBERNETES ON GOOGLE CLOUD

When you run a GKE cluster, you also gain the benefit of advanced cluster management features that Google Cloud provides. These include:

- Google Cloud's load-balancing for Compute Engine instances
- Node pools to designate subsets of nodes within a cluster for additional flexibility
- Automatic scaling of your cluster's node instance count
- Automatic upgrades for your cluster's node software
- Node auto-repair to maintain node health and availability
- Logging and monitoring with Google Cloud's operations suite for visibility into your cluster.

ReplicaSets

A ReplicaSet's purpose is to help maintain a stable set of replica Pods that runs at any time, such that, it is used often to guarantee the availability of a specific number of identical Pods.

The ReplicaSets can be said to be a grouping mechanism that Kubernetes uses to keep up the number of cases that have been pronounced for a given unit. The significance of a Replica Set uses a selector, whose evaluation will achieve distinguishing all units that are related to it.

Services

This is a simplified view in a Kubernetes cluster showing how Services interact with Pod networking.

A Kubernetes organization is a ton of pods that operates together, for example, one tier in a multi-tier application. A label selector defines the set of pods that constitute a service. There are two modes of service discovery that Kubernetes provides, using Kubernetes DNS using environmental variables or. Administration disclosure apportions a consistent IP address and DNS name to the organization, and weight alters traffic in a suitable method to mastermind relationship of that IP address among the cases coordinating the selector (even as disappointments cause the cases to move from machine to machine). Naturally, service is exposed inside a cluster (e.g., back end pods might be grouped into administration, with demands from the front-end cases load-adjusted among them); however, the administration can likewise be uncovered external a group (e.g., for customers to arrive at front-end cases).

Volumes

Filesystems provide temporary storage in the Kubernetes container; by default, this implies that a restart of the pod will erase any data on such containers. Therefore, this form of storage, although trivial in applications, is quite limiting in anything. For the lifetime of the pod, itself persistent storage that exists is provided by Kubernetes Volume. Containers within the pod use this storage as shared disk space for. Within the container at specific mount points volumes are mounted, which are defined by the pod configuration, and cannot mount onto other sizes or link to other formats. The same size can be installed in the filesystem tree by different containers at different points.

Namespaces

non-overlapping sets called namespaces are partitions of the resources Kubernetes provides, they are proposed for use in conditions with numerous clients spread over different groups, or extends, or in any event, isolating situations like a turn of events, test, and creation.

Configuration Maps and Secrets

where to store and manage configuration information is a common application challenge is deciding, some of which may contain delicate information. Setup information can be anything as fine-grained as individual properties or coarse-grained data like whole arrangement records or JSON/XML archives. Kubernetes gives two firmly related instruments to manage this need: "configmaps" and "mysteries", the two of which take into consideration design changes to be made without requiring an application construct. The information from setup guides and mysteries will be made accessible to every occurrence of the application to which these articles have been bound through the sending, if a pod on that node requires it only then will a Configuration map or a secret be sent to a node, Kubernetes will keep it in memory on that hub. When the pod that relies upon the mystery or configmap is erased, the in-memory duplicate of every single bound mystery and arrangement maps are taken out moreover. There are one of two different ways the information is open to the pod: (a) as domain factors (which will be made by Kubernetes when the pod is begun) or (b) accessible on the holder filesystem that is noticeable inside the pod.

The information itself is put away on the ace, which is a profoundly made sure about the machine which no one ought to have login admittance to, the most significant difference between a secret and a configuration map is that the substance of the information in mystery is base64 encoded. (On more up to date k8s forms, mysteries are put away scrambled in and so forth.)

StatefulSets

It is straightforward to address the scaling of stateless applications: one simply adds more running pods, which is something that Kubernetes does well overall. Stateful outstanding burdens are a lot harder because the state should be protected if a case is restarted, and if the application is scaled up or down, by then, the state may be redistributed. Information bases are a case of remaining stateful tasks at hand. At the point when run in high-accessibility mode, numerous information bases accompany the idea of an important occasion and an optional situation. In this case, the idea of the ordering of cases is essential. Other applications such as Kafka distribute the data amongst their brokers, so one intermediary isn't equivalent to another. For this situation, the idea of occurrence, uniqueness is fundamental. StatefulSets[30] are regulators (see Controller Manager, beneath) that are given by Kubernetes that uphold the properties of uniqueness and requesting among examples of a case and can be utilized to run stateful applications.

DaemonSets

The algorithm implemented in the Kubernetes Scheduler usually determines, the location where pods are run. For some use instances, there could be a need to run a pod on every single node in the cluster. It is use cases like ingress controllers, storage services, and log collection. The feature called DaemonSets enables the ability to do this kind of pod scheduling is implemented.

Secrets

Secrets contain the keys, passwords and OAuth tokens for the pod.

Managing Kubernetes objects

There are some mechanisms that Kubernetes provides, which allow one to select, manage, or even manipulate its objects.

Labels and selectors

clients(users or internal components) are enabled by Kubernetes to join keys called "names" to any API object in the framework, for example, cases and hubs. Correspondingly, "mark selectors" are inquiries against names that resolve to coordinate articles. Exactly when assistance is described, one can portray the name selectors that will be used by the organization switch/load balancer to pick the unit events that the traffic will be coordinated to, simply changing the signs of the cases or changing the name selectors on the organization can be used to control which cases get traffic and which don't, which can be used to help distinctive association plans like blue-green courses of action or A-B testing. This capacity to powerfully control how administrations use actualizing assets gives a free coupling inside the framework. All signs are highlighting Kubernetes turning into the defacto standard for compartment coordination stages, suppose you've done your examination, and you realize you need to utilize Kubernetes as your substance the board framework. Just fine. You additionally realize you have two principle cloud facilitating alternatives: Amazon Web Services (AWS) and Google Cloud Platform (GCP). Amazon's conspicuous decision, the same number of designers, have restricted presentation to and involvement in GCP and Google Container Engine (GKE).

Regardless, in case you have to run Kubernetes on AWS, you have a ton of work in front of you. In case you're searching for holder based work processes, GCP will make Kubernetes significantly simpler to oversee and stay up with the latest. Since Google made Kubernetes, GKE gives you a Kubernetes group out of the crate. As such, as opposed to setting up Kubernetes on AWS, there's a superior alternative: letting the individuals who manufactured Kubernetes likewise have it.

The Benefits Of Running Kubernetes On Google Container Engine

Kubernetes on GKE vs AWS

We should begin with the reason that it's smarter to run Kubernetes on GCP than on AWS. A rational inquiry to pose is the reason – what's the distinction?

The most direct answer is that Google plays a part in creating Kubernetes, so Google underpins new Kubernetes includes naturally and quicker – at times a whole lot faster than any other cloud providers. The Google Container Engine (GKE) supports the latest and most excellent versions of Kubernetes earlier than the other cloud providers.

You'll spend less time and money setting it up on Google than on AWS, If you know you want to use Kubernetes, then. Let's see what this means in real terms.

Closed vs Open Source

Amazon EC2 Container Service (ECS) is Amazon's endeavour to assemble a compartment group. It's altogether shut source, while Kubernetes is open source. You can see who's creating Kubernetes (and what they're making), and you're not secured in a cloud supplier (AWS or Google).

Uncommon vs Familiar Paradigms

Amazon has home-prepared its holder group programming, and the abilities you'll have to assemble when utilizing ECS are unique concerning those used on different stages. ECS is a mixed bag of Amazon's different administrations stuck together, which means it's neither vigorous nor architected such that makes it simple to use on creation outstanding burdens.

The skills you build with Kubernetes can be used on several other products and systems, whereas the skills you build using ECS is specialized and not appropriate to the greater part of the other work you do. Accordingly, running either ECS or Kubernetes on AWS will require a great deal of manual exertion, and you'll have to pay some dues.

Automation vs Manual Effort

In this way, if you have to utilize Kubernetes, GKE abbreviates the expectation to absorb information significantly because Google sets up its gauge usefulness for you. With GKE, you can turn on a Kubernetes group and be going in a short time, though on AWS you need to do a great deal of work to see how to set up the bunch, what tooling to utilize and how to construct the new group when you're prepared. You'll additionally need to investigate any issues that emerge and afterwards have the option to survey if the group is ready for action how you anticipated.

GKE wipes out these tedious advances. Simply disclose to GKE some fundamental things about your group, and it will amazingly bootstrap your bunch for you. GKE spares a huge amount of migraine and time in the genuine making of the bunch, and you can begin sending applications on the bunch rapidly without the overhead of keeping the group running in any case.

Simple vs Complex Integration

AWS doesn't have a managed Kubernetes installation as GKE does. GKE, then again, has Google backing and coordinates with the entirety of Google's other tooling. It accompanies worked in logging, logs the executives and observing at both the host and compartment levels. Not at all like AWS, it can give you programmed autoscaling, programmed equipment the executives and programmed variant updates. It, for the most part, gives you a prepared creation bunch with a greater number of batteries-included methodology than if you were building everything by hand on AWS.

The AWS/GCP Decision Is Yours

Network upholds for containerization groups is setting around Kubernetes. Since Kubernetes and GKE both grew inside Google, Google engineers are paid to help all Kubernetes includes sooner (and better) than other cloud administrations. Amazon isn't paying their specialists to make Kubernetes run better on Amazon.

With GKE, you prepare a creation Kubernetes bunch with all the essential tooling, alongside continuous help expected to ensure your bundles and forms remain current. GKE deals with security defaults for you and coordinates with other Google administrations. This blend requires less overhead in dealing with the bunch and makes it more consistent with using over the long haul.

Fairwinds can deal with Kubernetes on AWS and GCP. Either arrangement works fine and dandy for us. In any case, if you have the political capital and capacity to pick (if, for instance, you're not effectively an Amazon shop), GKE will make your life simpler.

Kubernetes is preferred on GKE over on AWS. Running Kubernetes on GCP will set aside your time and cash, just as give you a shorter expectation to absorb information, more cooperative energies.

Advantages Of Kubernetes

1. Using Kubernetes and its vast ecosystem can improve your productivity

If Kubernetes is appropriately implemented into your engineering workflows, it can lead to significant productivity gains. Especially the vast Kubernetes ecosystem, which can best be shown with the CNCF Landscape, helps to use Kubernetes effectively and proficiently lessening the negative effect of its overall intricacy. By depending on some current instruments explicitly made for cloud-local programming, you can get arrangements that you could scarcely ever construct yourself.

For instance: Our organization as of late included the open-source improvement device DevSpace to CNCF, which lets you set up and normalize the arrangement and testing work process for each designer in your group. Different instruments, for example, Drone allows you to rapidly make CI/CD pipelines for Kubernetes and devices like Prometheus, make observing more direct than any other time in recent memory. This plenty of devices accessible in the biological system abbreviate discharge cycles definitely, professionalizes designing work processes and inevitably improves the product quality from advancement to creation. This colossal choice of advances additionally causes you to redo everything precisely to your requirements. As an extra reward, the vast majority of the devices during the k8s environment are open-source and consequently allowed to utilize.

2. Kubernetes and a cloud-local tech stack draws inability

Numerous product engineers need to work in organizations that utilization current and energizing advances. Kubernetes is entirely one of them being positioned as the third most needed stages in the Stack Overflow Developer Survey 2019. Joined with a proficient work process with other cloud-local devices, your innovation stack and cycles will be alluring for possible candidates. Additionally, for your current workforce, it tends to be exceptionally propelling to work with something new, which improves the overall fulfilment in your dev groups and can even lessen representative turnover over the long haul. This favourable position of Kubernetes is regularly disregarded; however, given the deficiency of tech ability, it very well may be a material advantage for your association.

3. Kubernetes is a future confirmation arrangement

If you choose to make use of Kubernetes, you can be practically sure that this course of action is achievable for quite a while for a couple of reasons:

All significant cloud merchants are supporting Kubernetes giving out-of-the-case answers for it.

Elective holder organization arrangements are a long ways behind k8s as far as appropriation, uphold by cloud sellers and their biological systems. Indeed, even organizations recently centred around contending innovations are presently supporting Kubernetes: Docker is offering Docker Kubernetes Service rather than just Docker Swarm arrangements, and Mesosphere changed its name to D2IQ to be more open for Kubernetes and not merely centred around Apache Mesos.

What's more, obviously: The Kubernetes biological system is becoming amazingly quick, and new items supporting various needs on the head of the Kubernetes stage are being delivered each day.

Kubernetes is additionally future verification from an individual viewpoint: If you expect your client base to become even to an immense crowd, you can be sure that Kubernetes can deal with it since it is intended to help huge, circulated frameworks and it was initially evolved by Google designs and supported by their involvement with building adaptable stages like Borg. The equivalent goes for your application on the off chance that it develops and turns out to be more mind-boggling. Here, microservice structures frequently become possibly an essential factor, and for these, Kubernetes is the innovation of decision starting today. Lastly, if you need to switch your cloud seller for reasons unknown, for example moving from Amazon Web Services (AWS) to Microsoft Azure, you can without much of a stretch locate a fundamentally the same as

Kubernetes administration from an alternate supplier, and Kubernetes itself does such a switch generally consistent keeping you from merchant lock-in.

4. Kubernetes assists with making your application run more steady

On the off chance that you should be sure that your application is fully operational dependably, Kubernetes can uphold you in this. For instance, it permits you to have moving updates to change your product without personal time. It is further conceivable to set up Kubernetes such that it bolsters high accessibility applications. In case you are using the public cloud organizations of huge dealers, you can be almost sure to arrive at a high uptime. (In any case, this is additionally conceivable with different advances and frameworks yet frequently includes extensively more exertion.)

5. Kubernetes can be less expensive than its other options

Another favourable position of k8s is that it can at times be less expensive than different arrangements (contingent upon your application). Since the stage itself has some broad registering needs, it usually is more costly for little applications. Nonetheless, the bigger your figuring asset needs, the less important are these fundamental framework requirements for the general cost count. In such cases, different components become more significant. For instance, Kubernetes can auto-scale contingent upon the necessities of your application and the approaching traffic and burden prepared by your applications. That implies that Kubernetes can scale up your applications and its necessary assets during top occasions yet additionally downsize your framework during less active seasons, week or even hours of the day. That implies you save money if there isn't a lot of going on. In general, this prompts high use and keeps you from paying for assets that you needn't bother with.

The moderately new idea of "nodeless Kubernetes" with arrangements, for example, Virtual Kubelet or elot gives the extra potential to sparing framework cost.

By and large, Kubernetes would thus be able to be less expensive now and again and more costly in others, and there is consistently potential to lessen the expense of running it. For this, you have to assess it for your particular application and look at the changed suppliers for your requirements (be that as it may, for the decision of your cloud supplier, a greater number of elements than simply cost will, as a rule, assume a job).

Disadvantages Of Kubernetes

1. Kubernetes can be pointless excess for straightforward applications

Kubernetes is a complex however ground-breaking innovation that permits you to run the product in a cloud domain at a gigantic scope pretty productively. Notwithstanding, if you don't mean to create anything complex for an enormous or dispersed crowd (in this way, you are not building an overall online shop with a huge number of clients for instance) or with high figuring asset needs (for example AI applications), there isn't a lot of advantage for you from the specialized intensity of k8s. Suppose you simply need to build up a site demonstrating the opening times and area of your business. At that point you ought not to utilize Kubernetes because this isn't what it was made for; notwithstanding, one can't, for the most part, say that each AI programming should run with Kubernetes and no basic site should. It is merely far almost sure that it will be valuable in the primary case than in the other one.

2. Kubernetes is extremely mind-boggling and can lessen profitability

Kubernetes is scandalously known for its unpredictability. Particularly for engineers curious about framework advancements, it tends to be extremely difficult to work with; notwithstanding, on the off chance that you need to rehearse the DevOps approach, designers need to gain admittance to and send to Kubernetes as ahead of schedule as conceivable during the improvement lifecycle, so they can test their code rapidly and at an early stage to forestall exorbitant slip-ups later on underway. Even though there is an excellent propensity to make Kubernetes simpler and more open (DevSpace is, for instance, endeavouring to be the most agreeable and quickest Kubernetes device for designers), it is as yet fitting to have in any event one Kubernetes master with a significant comprehension of k8s on each building group. Somebody with this expertise can either be recruited, which is still generally costly - the average pay in the US for individuals with k8s abilities is more than $140,000, or be prepared, which will take some time.

Regardless, your advancement group should adjust a portion of its cycles to turn out to be truly cloud-local. In any event, temporarily, this may bring about decreased profitability and longer delivery cycles. (Notwithstanding, k8s can likewise help your profitability over the long haul, whenever done right)

3. The progress to Kubernetes can be bulky

Since most organizations can't begin a green field, your current programming should be adjusted to run easily with Kubernetes or possibly close by the recently fabricated application that will run on Kubernetes. It is difficult to assess how much exertion this requires as this relies intensely upon the product (for example is it previously containerized, which programming language is utilized). Furthermore, a few cycles should be adjusted to the new condition, particularly organization measures. Indeed, even with experienced staff nearby, the appropriation of Kubernetes may, in any case, be a test and requires very some exertion and time.

4. Kubernetes can be more costly than its other options

I have just depicted that Kubernetes can be less expensive than utilizing elective innovations. Notwithstanding, it can likewise be more costly, and this is because the entirety of the recently referenced drawbacks cost season of your architects that isn't spent on making new "substantial" business esteem.

If your designers are investing their energy getting a current, running application to run in Kubernetes, they will likely arrive at the norm with various innovation.

Also, on the off chance that they arrive at this objective, the clients of this application won't quickly observe any advantages of this movement (in any case, there may be some unpretentious points of interest, for example, improved solidness). Since building time is an exceptionally significant asset, this ought to be considered for your choice to receive Kubernetes.

Other than this aberrant expense, now and then the foundation cost of running Kubernetes is just higher than for elective frameworks, particularly for little applications as Kubernetes itself makes them register needs. Once more, taking the rearranged case of a basic site, it may very well be less expensive to pick a lot easier framework, for example, a solitary VM or facilitating stages, for example, Heroku or Netlify.

End

There is no simple answer if receiving Kubernetes is the correct decision for you or not. It relies upon your particular needs and needs, and numerous specialized reasons were not referenced here. If you are beginning with another task, if you work in a startup that plans to scale and needs to grow something beyond a fast MVP or if you have to redesign an inheritance application, Kubernetes may be a decent decision giving you a ton of adaptability, force and versatility.

In any case, it generally requires speculation of time because new abilities must be procured and new work processes must be set up in your dev group.

Whenever done right, notwithstanding, contributing an opportunity to learn and receive Kubernetes will frequently pay off later on because of better assistance quality, a higher efficiency level and a more inspired workforce.

Regardless, you should settle on an educated choice, and there are numerous valid justifications to go for Kubernetes or leave it. I trust this post will help you in drawing nearer to settling on the correct choice for you.

CHAPTER FIVE-
DESIGNING AND PLANNING A CLOUD SOLUTION ARCHITECTURE

There is quite a problem most cloud projects face that may cause them to fail and crash, and this happens as a result of wrong or missing architecture and design methods.

Usually, lack of a general understanding of methods that need to be applied to prepare suitable cloud computing solutions could lead the project to a rough end with developed problems like:

- Lack of governance and weak or no securities at all.
- Saturation of resources
- Inefficient utilization of resources
- Lack of scalability
- Lack of elasticity

A very solid cloud architecture design is reliable, and it forms a backbone of your cloud, and this begins with smart decisions made by you. A suitable and secure method of architecture design is required for taking advantage of the inherent strengths of cloud computing. Presently, cloud computing is quite different from what it was in the past [some years ago], and it will develop in a few years to come and more. The building or designing an effective cloud strategy today might save you the risks from tomorrow.

So, what are the emerging best methods and practices? What are the proper ways to leverage cloud computing systems? What are the proper techniques to build cloud computing systems? What are the appropriate ways to design cloud computing systems?

Well, just like many other IT architecture, there is no single solution. True, there are different situations and needs. Still, a good understanding of methods will save you from failing and pitfalls and will also help you evaluate your needs like Infrastructure, scalability, applications, security and compliance and as well build the proper cloud architecture. The best practices these days are around "fast planning".

Designing a Good Cloud Architecture

The following are common and best steps and practices you can employ to design your cloud architecture:

1. Multi-Cloud method: According to IDC Predictions of Worldwide Cloud in 2017, about 85% of Enterprise IT businesses in 2018 have committed to multi-cloud architectures; this commitment helped them to increase the rate and provided considerable opportunities to secure massive growth in their business field. Today, businesses need to seek help from one or multiple cloud-based service provider to provide security for their business data and other relevant information. Changing from one cloud to another could be possible if you make use of an excellent multi-cloud strategy. A good multi-cloud strategy will also ensure that you run the services balanced between two or more clouds. No one size automatically fits in all, through planning a multi-cloud method, you will comfortably perform tasks using the best performance ratio.

While engaging in the multi-cloud method, the following should be considered:

- An administration you may be getting with a cloud supplier may be performing better on the other. Critically check how services respond then create the right mixture for your business across multiple clouds.

- It is always a good thing to employ open-source replacements for any native service that you could replace. At start-up [in a short run], getting into a trap of native service will be easy but after experiencing expansion and growth in the long term, getting into such trap becomes difficult. When you use open-source replacements from the start, you experience suppleness with different services without being held and stuck with native services.

2. Optimize your cost: Cloud cost optimization strategy is a very comfortable and trusted way to reduce your overall cloud spends and reduce your cost to a minimum. With this strategy, you can spot and identify mismanaged resources, eliminating waste, and you can right-size computing services. The following steps will guide you in optimizing your cloud cost, and it is required you keep them in mind:

   - Have a defined baseline: Your starting point should be well defined and understood; something that will give you an awareness of situations. You can preferably use a tool like the free AWS Cost Explorer; this will help you A administration you may be getting with a cloud supplier may be macro and micro levels. Having a defined baseline will enable you to measure the impact of your optimization efforts over time.

- Right-Size your instances: According to Flexera 2020 State of the Cloud Report, A lot of organizations right-size their cases. Right-sizing your case is a primary way of controlling cloud costs.

Spot instances, Reserve instances and Saving plans are three best right-sizing tactics.

Spot instances are less expensive, and it offers the greatest savings. Here, the cloud provider does not commit to providing the case at a specified time. You can comfortably choose what you would like to run and the duration as well. Spot instances are ideal and recommended for flexible workloads like batch processing.

For Reserve instances and saving plans, they offer similar sized savings at up to 72% or so. Regardless of their differences, their similarity is a steep discount in exchange for a single or multi-year commitment to the platform.

As workloads change, instance needs will change too. Therefore, for instance, right-sizing should be an ongoing exercise and not just a single or once approach.

- Another way you can reduce cost in selecting the right types, configurations and storage solutions to suit your needs. There is no extra cost in implementing auto-scaling to be able to scale when required horizontally or to scale down when necessary.

- Reduce the cost of data transfer: One of the things you should know is that Data transfer is free in the same region. Therefore, you should ensure that your Object storage and Computer Services are in the same area. For example, to download the file a file from another AWS region, AWS will charge $0.02/GB.

It might be less expensive to reproduce your Object Storage container to an alternate district utilizing an element incorporated with S3 called cross-area replication. It will empower you to improve execution alongside money-saving advantage.

Let me expand your understanding using the AWS S3's example. Take, for instance, 1GB data in location"B" is anticipated to be transferred 20 times to EC2 in location "A". On the off chance that you start between district move, you will pay about $0.20 for information move [20 * 0.02]. Nevertheless, if you at first download it to reflect S3 pail in the area "An", at that point you will simply need to pay $0.02 for a move and pay $0.03 for capacity longer than a month, and it is 75% less expensive.

Compress Data Before Storage: Compressing information lessens your capacity prerequisites and subsequently reduces the cost of storage. A comfortable and less stressful way is to use a fast compression algorithm. A preferable algorithm to use is LZ4; it is a lossless compression algorithm which provides pressure speed at 400 MB/s percenter [0.16 Bytes/cycle]. It also features a high-speed decoder, with speed in, multiple GB/s per core [0.71 Bytes/cycle].

3. Operational Excellence: One thing that drives excellence is a significant operation. To accomplish this, you ought to have the option to manage workloads. These are procedures and practices you should follow to manage workloads:

- Align processes – Operations should be automated with codes.

- Collect metrics from various resources and then align processes on the business needs.

- Make Incremental Changes – To avoid failure in cases of unexpected events and to identify and get rid of the cause, you should make small incremental changes instead of making changes in big packages.

- Unexpected events – For sure, unforeseen circumstances may arise; always test for unforeseen circumstances. Capture events and failures too and then design a room for improvements.

- Maintain documentation – Always keep your procedures and documentation up to date and avoid any form of delay, which may be useful for understanding and troubleshooting purposes.

4. Performance/Efficiency: A lot of performance benefits could be achieved if you design your environment with the correct stage and in the right manner. But the question is, how efficiently you can manage your computer resources to meet your requirements?

   These are four steps that you can follow to manage to compute resources:

   - Make use of Latest Technologies –Your applications and services should be built on an evolved platform. High performances environment and templates can give you an advantage of a better performing cloud.

   - Right-sized – You should choose the right services and observe your environment, studying what services are best suitable to match what you demand.

- Put automation in place. When you implement automation and put automation in place, you get the ability to experiment more often and minimize manual processes.

- Listen to your application –based on your evolving requirements, a cloud service you chose yesterday might not be the best today. Identify and know your applications resource requirements such as RAM, CPU, Storage, etc.

5. Reliability: Before architecting your cloud, you should ensure to take on the best practices. Your starting should be reliable. Your framework ought to be able to recoup from the outage and be able to meet demands dynamically. Your system should effectively and technically work in every scenario. Ensure you follow the following practices:

    - You should critically think of how you can recover from failure quickly. A proper approach to this is to design an automated recovery process and as well as anticipate failures. You should be aware of how failures would happen and how well you can respond to failures when they come up.

    - Do not share a specific purpose of disappointment and set up repetitive engineering to evade personal time plan exceptionally accessible engineering.

    - Stick to processes and follow them. You should always create a strategy to make any changes in monolithic architecture, covering changes in demand, monitoring resources and executing.

- Stop guessing capacity – The idea of guessing can either produce under-provision or over-provision. Thinking will lead you to either have an outage, or your systems may be left sitting idle.

- Make use of a redundant network. This will have you eliminate network failures.

6. Proactive Planning: Just like the famous saying goes "prevention is better than cure", always have a theory that your hardware will fail and follow such theory. Have a mechanism to deal with unknown failures and catastrophes before it affects you.

   You should be able to consider the following practices:

   - Don't predict your capacity – Avoid guessing and predicting your capacity. A wrong prediction might lead you to expensive resources, or you might have to deal with performance implications of limited size.

   - Automate – You can create and replicate systems with automation; this will make your architecture dynamic. Automation reduces the risk of design changes.

   - Be data-driven – Your data will inform you of the choice you need to make. In the cloud, you can gather information on the behaviour of your application needs and identify what's best.

   - Design Evolutionary Architecture – An evolutionary architecture enable changes in architecture over time. Quick changes in a business domain could impede the choices to convey, however following prescribed procedures and implementing them while designing cloud architecture can help you evolve.

7. Security: Securing your cloud environment should be your primary concern, especially when you are running your apps on a cloud or when you are migrating to another cloud. Cloud security is just everything! You don't just think security at critical levels and in time of failing. Your safety should be hardened at all layers. Your Cloud and data could be affected by unauthorized actions and operations when it's not secured and protected. That is why you must discover and harden your securities layers. Some ways to learn and ensure protection for your cloud environment are:

    - Protect your Data - Closely observe and focus on your data protection.

      *Data should be classified in different segments. For example, the Public segment, the private segment, shared, etc.

      *Hide your data. You can achieve this by creating code or something private. Your data should be well encrypted.

      *Create different policies to prevent Accidental and unplanned overwrites and changes.

    - Take a detailed assessment of your infrastructure from policies to patches ensuring your infrastructure is secured and protected. These are good and better practices to this approach:

      * Use antivirus and firewalls to ensure your foundation and harden your security with all individual OS patches regularly.

      * Periodic checks and Traceability – Always take on periodic checks and identify loop-holes. Check the

ports, the layers and trace on how someone can hack into an environment.

- Follow Access Specifiers – In as much as you are responsible for securing your data, OS and application, it is always advisable that you do not use admin or root logins unless they are required. Even if it is necessary, you must do the following:

  * Create password logging policies for yourself.

  * Use keys Management services

  * Enable multi-factor authentication

  *You should also limit access to your data or your apps from other apps or 3rd party tools.

  * Assign least privilege access system

8. Automate Security: Cloud enables automation of several events which improves both your system's stability and the efficiency of your organization. You should have an awareness of everything and be responsible for all the security events such as 2FA, SSH, encryption, authenticity etc. Perhaps the most certain activity while moving quickly is to test and review your condition. You can execute persistent observing and mechanization of controls to limit the presentation to security hazards.

9. Your security should be automated at all events. To do this, you can set notifications or set emails whenever someone accesses the cloud.

10. Caching: This is one approach that can boost your application performance and cost-efficiency of an application. Caching is

a simple method or technique of storing in your memory, data and information that are used frequently so that if the same data or information is needed in next operation, you could directly retrieve it from memory instead of it being generated by the application. Caching is similar to storing state objects. However, the storing information in state objects is deterministic, i.e., you can comfortably count on the data being stored there but caching of data is nondeterministic.

Applying information storing to numerous layers of your cloud architecture will give you the best application performance you will need.

There are three types of caching; they include Edge Caching, Application Data Caching and Distributed Caching.

- Edge caching: With this, contents are served by infrastructures that are closer to the viewers lowering latency and also offer you the high, sustained data transfer you will need to deliver large popular objects to end users at scale.

- Application data caching: Application data caching will help your application load faster and give your users a better experience. With this, information can be stored and retrieved from fast, managed, in-memory caches in the application, and this decreases load for the database and increases the latency for end-users as mentioned earlier, that caching of data is non-deterministic. The information won't be accessible in the following cases:

  * If the lifetime of the data expires,

  * If the application releases its memory,

* If the caching process does not take place for some reasons.

The primary reason for caching is to reduce the cost of data access, and this can mean either: Monetary costs, for example, paying for the volume of data sent or bandwidth, or then again Opportunity costs, such as preparing time that could be utilized for different purposes.

- Distributed Caching: This is mainly used to store application data residing in database and web session data. Several high volume systems like Google, Amazon, YouTube and many others make use of this technique. This technique allows the web servers to pull and store from distributed server's memory. When this technique is applied, it will enable the web-server to simply serve pages without the fear of running out of memory. It will allow the distributed cache to be made up of a cluster of cheaper machines only serving up memory. Immediately the cluster is set up; you can begin to add a new device of memory at any time without disrupting your users.

Have you ever thought about how huge organizations like Google could return results so quickly,

When they have thousands of sequential users? Well, this is because they use Clustered Distributed Caching along with other methods to infinitely store the data in memory because memory retrieval is faster than file or DB retrieval.

11. Make sure you remove the single point of failure: Systems are highly available when they can endure the failure of single or multiple components like servers, network links, hard disks, etc.

The following processes will guide you through automating the recovery and reducing disruption at every layer of your cloud architecture:

- Introduce redundancy – This will have you eliminate single purposes of disappointment by having numerous assets for a similar assignment. Repetition can be executed in either reserve mode or active mode. With the standby mode, Functionality is recovered through failover while the resources remain unavailable. While in the active mode, requests are distributed to multiple redundant compute resources. If one of them eventually fails, the rest of them can simply absorb a larger share of the workload.

- Both Identification and reaction to failure should be automated as much as possible.

- It is imperative to have a durable data storage that protects both the availability of data and integrity. Redundant copies of data can be introduced by either synchronous, asynchronous or Quorum based replication.

12. Think Elastic and Adaptive: Cloud architecture is expected to support the growth of users or data size with no drop in performance because there will be growth in these areas. The cloud architecture should also allow for linear scalability when and where an additional resource is added.

    Your design should be equipped to take advantage of the virtually unlimited on-demand capacity of cloud computing.

    For instance, if you are building cloud architecture for short term purpose, you can implement vertical scaling. If the vertical scaling is not applied, you should convey your outstanding burden to different assets to assemble web-scale applications by scaling evenly. In any case, your cloud architecture should be elastic enough to adapt to the demands of cloud computing.

Also, to have your cloud very effective in storage, you should know when to connect with stateless applications, stateful applications, stateless segments and dispersed processing.

CHAPTER SIX - MANAGING AND PROVIDING THE CLOUD SOLUTION INFRASTRUCTURE

Cloud infrastructure is extensive and complex. It refers to the servers, software, network devices, and storage devices that make up the cloud. Cloud foundation additionally incorporates a reflection layer that virtualizes assets presents them to users through application program interfaces and APL – enabled command line or graphic interfaces. It's no different from typical data centre infrastructure except that it's virtualized and consumed over the Internet.

Beyond data centres, distributed computing has been a progressive innovation pattern for organizations of all sizes across for all intents and purposes each industry, and it's become a central part of a cutting edge biological system and application mix methodology. Rather than putting resources into exorbitant equipment while overseeing and keep up a server farm in-house, organizations are going to cloud suppliers like Amazon Web Services, Google Cloud, and Microsoft Azure for adaptable cloud framework to give modernized registering systems administration, and capacity thinks about distributed computing.

Cloud and storage infrastructure falls into three categories – computing, networking.

Cloud infrastructure management is the setup, configuration, monitoring, and optimization of the components of cloud infrastructure. This cloud infrastructure management happens through a web-based interface. Cloud infrastructure management gives enterprises some level of scalability and consolidates IT resources.

Cloud foundation comprises of workers, stockpiling gadgets, organization, cloud the executives programming, arrangement programming, and stage virtualization.

Distributed computing framework parts

1. Hypervisor

The hypervisor is a firmware or low-level program that goes about as a Virtual Machine Manager. It permits us to share the single physical occasion of cloud assets between a few inhabitants.

2. Management Software

It assists with keeping up and arrange the framework.

3. Deployment Software

It helps with sending and incorporate the application on the cloud.

4. Network

The organization is a vital part of a cloud foundation. It permits associating cloud administrations over the Internet. It is likewise conceivable to convey the organization as a utility over the Internet, which implies, the client can alter the organization course and convention.

5. Server

The worker assists with figuring the asset sharing and offers different administrations, for example, asset distribution and de-allotment, checking the assets, giving security and so on.

6. Storage

Cloud keeps various reproductions of capacity. If one of the capacity assets falls flat, at that point, it tends to be separated from another, which makes distributed computing more dependable.

7. Infrastructural Constraints

Major requirements that cloud framework should execute have appeared in the accompanying graph:

Distributed computing Infrastructure Constraints

a. Transparency

Virtualization is the best approach to share resources in a cloud space. Be that as it may, it is beyond the realm of imagination to expect to fulfil the interest with a solitary asset or worker. In this manner, there must be straightforwardness in assets, load adjusting and application, with the goal that we can scale them on request.

b. Scalability

Scaling up an application conveyance arrangement isn't that simple as scaling up an application since it includes design overhead or even re-architecting the organization. Thus, an application conveyance arrangement should have been adaptable, which will require the virtual foundation with the end goal that asset can be provisioned and de-provisioned without any problem.

c. Intelligent Monitoring

The application solution delivery will need to be capable of intelligent monitoring, and this will help achieve transparency and scalability

d. Security

The super server farm in the cloud ought to be safely architected. Likewise, the control hub, a passage point in the uber server farm, should be secure.

An oversaw administration is a basic asset that consistently speaks to assistance incorporated with Service Infrastructure, for example, Gmail API and Spanner API. A led administration itself has just two permanent properties, a help name and a maker venture; however, the execution of an oversaw administration can give a broad scope of usefulness. For instance, Cloud Storage API provides planet-scale object stockpiling to a large number of engineers and ventures.

An oversaw administration has a lot of administration shoppers, a past filled with unchanging help arrangements, and a background marked by permanent assistance rollouts. The administration arrangements referred to by the most recent assistance rollout speaks to the present status of the administration, which covers all parts of the administration, from the showcase name to measurements definitions as far as possible. For the detail, see google.api.Service.

We will depict how to make and deal with your administration lifecycles on this page. For more data about the assistance the executives, perceive How-to Guides.

Making help

To make help, you have to finish the accompanying advances.

I. Install and instate Cloud SDK on your PC

II. Create a committed maker undertaking to have your administration. A devoted implementation gives the best security and confinement for your administration. It additionally permits you to move the responsibility for administration to another group or much another organization.

III. Enable Cloud Billing for your venture. To incorporate your administration with Service Infrastructure, you will rely upon a few paid Google Cloud items, including the Service Control API, Cloud Logging API, and Cloud Monitoring API.

IV. Prepare a basic assistance setup document for your administration as folio Run cloud command to create your service by deploying a new service configuration:

Cloud endpoints administrations convey endpointsapis.yaml

The administration creation measure takes about a moment. Beginning now and for a significant length of time, you should have the choice to see your association recorded on the Endpoints page in Google Cloud Console.

Listing organizations

To list administrations in an undertaking, you can utilize the accompanying order:

cloud endpoints services list --project endpoints

Describing a service

Requirements for Building a Cloud Infrastructure

When building out a cloud strategy, several in-depth steps must be taken to guarantee a robust framework.

Requirements 1: Service and Resource Management

A cloud framework virtualizes all parts of a server farm. Administration, the executives, is a deliberate bundle of uses and administrations that end clients can without much of a stretch send and oversee through open and private cloud merchant. Also, a disentangled apparatus to framework and measure administrations is fundamental for cloud heads to showcase usefulness. Administration, the executives, need to contain asset support, asset ensures, charging cycles, and estimated guidelines. Once conveyed, the executives' administrations should help make arrangements for information and work processes to ensure it's completely productive, and measures are related to frameworks in the cloud.

Requirements 2: Data Center Management Tools Integration

Most server farms use an assortment of IT instruments for frameworks the board, security, provisioning, client care, charging, and registries, among others. Also, these work with cloud the executives' administrations and open APIs to coordinate existing activity, organization, support, and provisioning (OAM&P) frameworks. A cutting edge cloud administration should uphold a server farm's current foundation just as utilizing progressed programming, equipment, and virtualization, and other innovation.

Requirement 3: Reporting, Visibility, Reliability, and Security

Server farms need elevated levels of constant announcing and permeability capacities in cloud situations to ensure consistency, SLAs, security, charging, and chargebacks. Without powerful revealing and permeability, overseeing framework execution, client support, and different cycles are almost inconceivable. Furthermore, to be entirely reliable, cloud foundations must work paying little mind to at least one bombing segments, to shield the cloud, administrations must guarantee information and applications are secure while giving admittance to the individuals who are approved.

Requirement 4: Interfaces for Users, Admins, and Developers

Mechanized arrangement and self-administration interfaces ease complex cloud administrations for end-clients, helping lower working expenses and convey reception. Self-administration interfaces offer clients the capacity to successfully dispatch a cloud administration by dealing with their own server farm s, planning and driving formats, keeping up virtual capacity, organizing assets, and using libraries. Administrative interfaces present better permeability to all assets, virtual machines, models, administration offers, and different cloud clients. And these structures coordinate by a method of APIs for designers.

Cloud Infrastructure use Advantages

As technology continues to improve, the arguments in favour of using the cloud are only getting stronger. Thus, there are some undeniable key advantages in moving to a cloud framework that assists organizations with smoothing out business measures.

Cost: First and preeminent, the cloud eliminates or incredibly diminishes the operational cost of an organization setting up and dealing with its information, with all the diverse equipment, programming, workers, vitality charges, IT specialists, and the updates that come together with this multi-faceted set-up taking on this procedure starts to add up. With cloud infrastructure, while paying only for as-needed services, a company simply pays for it all to be managed

Agility and flexibility: Most cloud administration foundations are offered as self-guided, where administration changes can be made in practically no time, this improves the uptime and proficiency of business frameworks while permitting off-site collaborators and accomplices to get to shared information on cell phones at whatever point and any place. Furthermore, with a cloud foundation overseeing measures, an organization turns out to be more business-centred than IT-centered.

Security: There's a typical confusion that cloud administrations are commonly not secure and that information can without much of a stretch be undermined. There is a trace of authenticity in that. In any case, the risks are often made a tremendous arrangement about at any rate concerning wander level cloud establishment and organizations. Cloud framework innovations and suppliers are continually improving insurance against programmers, infections, and other information penetrates with more powerful firewalls, progressed encryption keys, and a crossover approach that stores delicate information in a private cloud and other information, even applications, in a public cloud.

Disadvantages of Using Cloud Infrastructure

That being stated, not all cloud frameworks are great. And keeping in mind that there are unmistakably more preferences, there are still a few disadvantages.

Seller upsets: The cloud is as yet developing, though improving, an innovation that quickly varies. Which means, some cloud administrations organizations hit the nail on the head, and some don't. If an organization leaves the business or sees a monstrous update, that could be dangerous to a business that depends on only one foundation for its whole information base.

Association dependence: A cloud framework is just equivalent to its organization association. Consequently, the cloud can't remain above water without a reliable association. Any glitches in a web or intranet association because of a specialized blackout or tempest mean the cloud goes down alongside all the information, programming, and applications in it. A dependable organization implies business guarantees and SLAs are conveyed.

Its service provider generally controls control: Since a company's cloud infrastructure, there are times organizations have limited access to data. And business customers have even less power than they might want, with limited access to applications, data, and tools stored on a server.

Basic Requirements For Effective Cloud Infrastructure Management

THERE ARE BASIC REQUIREMENTS FOR EFFECTIVE CLOUD INFRASTRUCTURE MANAGEMENT

SERVICE MANAGEMENT

Productizing cloud functionality requires administrators to have the right tools for the definition and metering of service offerings. A service offering is a set of applications and services that end-users can consume on both public and private clouds.

Private cloud foundation is worked for a solitary association. A third party can internally manage it. Individual cloud systems can provide flexible storage capacity and computing power for different areas of business. Still, they lack the element of management that makes cloud computing an attractive economic model for leveraging IT infrastructure. A service offering should ideally include metering rules, guarantees, resource management, and billing cycles. Service management functionality must have a link to the broader offering repository; this makes it easier for the user to deploy and manage defined services.

Public cloud administrations are conveyed over an organization that is open for public use. They can give unbending capacity limit. With this sort of cloud, people, in general, can buy or rent information stockpiling or registering limit varying.

VISIBILITY AND REPORTING

It is one of the key segments of the cloud framework of the board. We realize that security is among the top, if not the top worry for CIOs when settling on choices about moving remaining burdens into the cloud. Without permeability into your information, it's hard if not difficult to investigate, to determine administration issues and to make sure that security controls are working. So because of that, it becomes impossible to monitor customer service levels, compliance, system performance, and billing. Real-time visibility and monitoring give administrators the ability to manage compliance, security, billing, and other instruments seamlessly. They require high levels of granular visibility and reporting.

From a business point of view, this all bodes well regarding decreasing expectations to absorb information and stopped issues from really developing before they become major, income influencing cataclysms.

Be that as it may, checking can likewise conceal into an examination, which can include business esteem. This implies permitting you to distinguish patterns in application execution and conduct, recognize utilization examples, and answers to inquiries regarding site execution.

So cloud frameworks the board isn't just about watching out for frameworks and reacting to cautions. Like any type of proactive support, as utilized progressively by organizations in all sections, it's tied in with empowering the capacity to turn out to be more client-centred, more agile and adaptable, and reducing the expenses of overseeing foundation.

If a cloud supplier isn't conveying on this front, they do not include enough worth. The director of Professional Services at Rackspace, Adam Evans, prompts that associations, post-movement, manufacture an objective working model that accept change is the new trend.

"Accept that you will continually be devouring innovations, at that point assemble better cycles to evaluate and bring them ineffectually, this will assist you with conveying more noteworthy business esteem from these speculations and abstain from overburdening yourself with dealing with the developing cloud spread."

INTEGRATION WITH DATA CENTER MANAGEMENT TOOLS

Most occasions, you should coordinate new cloud the board arrangements with parts of inheritance information centres. Legacy data centres have a variety of tools used for provisioning, billing, customer service, systems management, security, directory, and others. Cloud infrastructure management solutions don't replace these tools. It's, therefore, essential to have APIs that integrate into existing OAM&P (operation, administration, maintenance, and provisioning) systems.

Data management is the spine that connects all segments of the information lifecycle.

Data management refers to the professional practice of constructing and maintaining a framework for ingesting, storing, mining, and archiving data integral to modern business. Data management is the spine that connects all segments of the information lifecycle.

Data management works symbiotically with process management, ensuring that the actions teams take are informed by the cleanest, most current data available—which, today, means tracking changes and trends in real-time. Below is a more in-depth look at the practice, its benefits and challenges, and the best practices for helping your organization get the most out of its business intelligence.

END-USER, DEVELOPER, AND ADMINISTRATOR USER INTERFACES

Self-service portals and deployment models help shield the end-user from the complexity of the cloud, and this helps drive adoption and decreases operating costs since the end-user takes up most management tasks. The user can manage his or her virtual data centre, manage virtual storage, and create and launch templates. The user can also access image libraries and manage the network and compute resources.

Administrators should get a UI that gives them a single-pane view of all cloud resources. They should see virtual machine instances, physical resources, service offerings, templates, and users. Developers should also access all these features through standard APIs.

DYNAMIC RESOURCE AND WORKLOAD MANAGEMENT

The cloud must be resource and workload aware. Then, it will be truly on-demand and elastic and meet SLAs (service level agreements). Cloud computing virtualizes all data centre components. The resultant abstraction requires cloud infrastructure management solutions that can create policies around workload and data management. It ensures maximum performance and efficiency for the applications running in the cloud, and it is particularly essential when systems hit peak demand. The system should dynamically prioritize resources on the fly depending on the enterprises' priorities or various workloads.

Cloud resource management has been a critical factor for cloud data centres development. Many cloud datacentres have issues in comprehension and executing the strategies to oversee, distribute and relocate the assets in their premises. The outcomes of inappropriate asset the executives may result in underutilized and wastage of assets which may likewise bring about helpless assistance conveyance in these datacentres. Assets like, CPU, memory, Hard plate and workers should be all around recognized and oversaw. In this Paper, Dynamic Resource Management Algorithm (DRMA) will restrict itself in the administration of CPU and memory as the assets in cloud server farms. The objective is to spare those assets which might be underutilized at a specific period. It very well may be accomplished through Implementation of reasonable calculations. Here, Bin pressing algorithm can be utilized whereby the best-fit algorithm is sent to acquire results and contrasted with select a fitting algorithm for effective utilization of assets.

Cloud Management Tasks

The cloud supplier plays out a few assignments to guarantee the effective utilization of cloud assets. Here, we will examine some of them:

Cloud Management Tasks

Review System Backups

It is needed to review the reinforcements convenient to guarantee the reestablishing of haphazardly chosen records of various clients. Reinforcements can be acted in the following:

Backing up documents by the organization, from on-location PCs to the circles that live inside the cloud.

Backing up documents by the cloud supplier.

It is important to know whether the cloud supplier has encoded the information, which approaches that information and if the reinforcement is taken in various areas. The client must know the subtleties of those areas.

Data Flow of the System

The administrators are answerable for building up an outline portraying a point by point measure stream. This cycle stream depicts the development of information having a place with an association all through the cloud arrangement.

Vendor Lock-In Awareness and Solutions

The administrators must realize the method to exit from administrations of a specific cloud supplier. The strategies must be characterized to empower the cloud administrators to trade information of an association from their framework to another cloud supplier.

Knowing Provider's Security Procedures

The directors should realize the security plans of the supplier for the following administrations:

- Encryption policy
- Employee screening
- Multitenant use

E-commerce processing

Monitoring Capacity Planning and Scaling Capabilities

The managers must know the capacity planning to guarantee whether the cloud supplier is meeting the future limit prerequisite for his business or not.

The supervisors must deal with the scaling capacities to guarantee administrations can be scaled up or down according to the client need.

Monitor Audit Log Use

To distinguish mistakes in the framework, directors must review the logs consistently.

Solution Testing and Validation

When the cloud provider provides a solution, it is necessary to test it to guarantee that it gives the right outcome and it is without mistake, this is fundamental for a framework to be strong and reliable.

CHAPTER SEVEN - SECURITY DESIGN AND COMPLIANCE FOR CLOUD SOLUTION

Introduction

Security Architecture and Design talks about fundamental logical hardware, operating system, and software security components and how to use those components to architect, design, and evaluate secure computer systems. Understanding these fundamental issues is reproving for an information security professional.

Cloud compliance is all about complying with the rules and regulations that apply to use the cloud. Most organizations are moving to the cloud because there are more advantages and benefits to do so. The law does not prevent the adoption of the cloud. It does, however, have a significant impact, it is essential to know in which countries your data will be processed when moving to the cloud; what laws will apply, what impact they will have, and then follow a risk-based approach to comply with them, this can be exceptionally bothersome because there are a broad scope of kinds of laws, similar to information limitation law, information assurance law and information sway laws. You also need to consider interception laws or access to information laws, which may enable Governments or others to access your data in the cloud. Also, the laws of many different countries might apply. It is likewise significant that you know which security measures the law requires you to put in place.

We will just go ahead to look into the different features of how google cloud handles their security designs for cloud infrastructure.

Google security for physical speculation

Google plans and manufactures its server farms, which consolidate various layers of physical security assurances. Admittance to these server farms is restricted to just a little part of Google representatives. They utilize different physical security layers to ensure our server farm floors and use innovations like distinguishing biometric proof, metal location, cameras, vehicle obstructions, and laser-based interruption recognition frameworks. Google furthermore has a few workers in third-gathering server farms, where we guarantee that there are Google-controlled physical safety efforts on the head of the security layers gave by the server farm administrator. For instance, in such locales, we may work autonomous biometric distinguishing proof frameworks, cameras, and metal locators.

Hardware Design

A Google server farm comprises of thousands of worker machines associated with a nearby organization. Google handcrafts both the worker sheets and the systems administration hardware. They choose component vendors they work with and choose components with care while working with vendors to audit and confirm the security operations which is provided by the elements. They additionally plan custom chips, including an equipment security chip that is right now being sent on the two workers and peripherals. These chips permit us to safely distinguish and validate authentic Google gadgets at the equipment grade or degree.

Secure Boot Stack and Machine Identity

Google worker machines utilize an assortment of advancements to guarantee that they are booting the right programming stack. We use cryptographic marks over low-level segments like the BIOS, bootloader, portion, and base working framework picture. These marks can be approved during each boot or update. The parts are all

Google-controlled, assembled, and solidified. With each new age of equipment, we endeavour to improve security ceaselessly: for instance, contingent upon the period of worker plan, we root the trust of the boot chain in either a lockable firmware chip, a microcontroller running Google-composed security code, or the previously mentioned Google-planned security chip.

Every worker machine in the server farm has its particular character that can be attached to the equipment foundation of trust and the product with which the machine booted. This personality is utilized to validate API calls to and from low-level administration administrations on the device.

Google has created mechanized frameworks to guarantee workers approach date renditions of their product stacks (counting security patches), to identify and analyze equipment and programming issues, and to eliminate machines from administration if vital.

Secure Service Deployment

We will currently proceed to portray how we go from the base equipment and programming to guaranteeing that assistance is conveyed safely on our foundation. By 'administration' we mean an application parallel that an engineer composed and needs to run on our framework, for instance, a Gmail SMTP worker, a Bigtable stockpiling worker, a YouTube video transcoder, or an App Engine sandbox running a client application. There might be a great many machines running duplicates of similar assistance to deal with the necessary size of the remaining task at hand. Administrations running on the foundation are constrained by a bunch organization administration called Borg.

As we will find in this segment, google foundation doesn't expect any trust between administrations running on the framework. As such, the framework is essentially intended to be multi-occupant.

Service Identity, Integrity, and Isolation

We utilize cryptographic confirmation and approval at the application layer for between administration correspondence. Gives significant access control at a reflection level and granularity that executives and administrations can normally comprehend.

We don't depend on inner organization division or firewalling as our essential security instruments. In any case, we do utilize entrance and departure separating at different focuses in our organization to forestall IP satirizing as a further security layer. This methodology additionally encourages us to amplify our organization's presentation and accessibility.

Each help that sudden spikes in demand for the framework have a related assistance account character. The administration is given cryptographic qualifications that it can use to demonstrate its personality when making or accepting remote system calls (RPCs) to different administrations. These characters are utilized by customers to guarantee that they are conversing with the right expected worker, and by workers to restrict admittance to techniques and information to specific customers.

Google's source code is put away in a focal vault where both current and past adaptations of the administration are auditable. The framework can moreover be designed to necessitate that an assistance's doubles be worked from explicit inspected, checked in, and tried source code. Such code surveys require examination and endorsement from at any rate one architect other than the creator, and the framework upholds that the proprietors must affirm code alterations to any arrangement of that framework. These prerequisites limit the capacity of an insider or foe to make noxious changes to source code and give a criminological path from administration back to its source.

They have a different species of isolation and sandboxing techniques for protecting a service from other services running on the same machine. These techniques include normal separation, language and kernel-based sandboxes, and hardware virtualization. By and large, they utilize more layers of disconnection for more dangerous remaining tasks at hand; for instance, when running complex record design converters on client-provided information or when running client provided code for items like Google App Engine or Google Compute Engine. As an additional security limit, we empower exceptionally delicate administrations, for example, the group arrangement administration and some key administration administrations, to run only on devoted machines.

Between Service Access Management

The proprietor of help can utilize access the executives' highlights gave by the foundation to determine precisely which different administrations can speak with it. For instance, assistance might need to offer some APIs exclusively to a particular whitelist of different administrations. That administration can be designed with the whitelist of the permitted administration account characters, and this entrance limitation is then consequently implemented by the foundation.

Google engineers getting to administrations are additionally given individual characters, so administrations can be likewise arranged to permit or deny their gets to. These kinds of characters (machine, administration, and representative) are in a worldwide namespace that the infrastructure keeps up, will be made clear later in this report, end-client characters are dealt with independently.

The foundation gives a beneficial personality the executives work process framework for these inside characters, including endorsement chains, logging, and warning. For instance, these personalities can be doled out to get to control bunches through a framework that permits two gathering controls where one designer can propose a change to a gathering that another architect (who is likewise a director of the community) must affirm. This framework permits secure access to the executives' cycles to scale to a great many administrations running on the foundation.

Notwithstanding the programmed API-level access control system, the foundation likewise offers types of assistance with the capacity to peruse from focal ACL and gathering information bases so they can execute their custom, fine-grained admittance control where essential.

Encryption of Inter-Service Communication

Past the RPC verification and approval capacities examined in the past areas, the framework likewise gives cryptographic security and uprightness to RPC information on the organization. To provide these security advantages to other application-layer conventions, for example, HTTP, we epitomize them inside our framework RPC components. Generally, this gives application layer disengagement and eliminates any reliance on the security of the organization way. Scrambled between administration correspondence can stay secure regardless of whether the organization is tapped or an organization gadget is undermined.

Administrations can rebuild the degree of cryptographic security they need for every framework RPC (for example just design trustworthiness level assurance for low-esteem information inside server farms). To secure against refined foes who might be attempting to tap our private WAN connections, the framework consequently encodes all foundation RPC traffic which goes over the WAN between server farms, without requiring any express design from the administration. We have begun to send equipment cryptographic quickening agents that will permit us to stretch out this default encryption to all foundation RPC traffic inside our server farms.

Access Management of End User Data

An average Google administration is composed to accomplish something for an end-client. For instance, an end-client may store their email on Gmail. The end client's connection with an application like Gmail ranges different administrations inside the foundation. In this way, for instance, the Gmail administration may call an API given by the Contacts administration to get to the end client's location book.

We have found in the first segment that the Contacts administration can be arranged with the end goal that the main RPC demands that are permitted are from the Gmail administration (or from whatever other specific administrations that the Contacts administration needs to empower). Notwithstanding, this is as yet a broad arrangement of consents. Inside the extent of this authorization, the Gmail administration would have the option to demand the contacts of any client whenever.

Since the Gmail administration makes an RPC solicitation to the Contacts administration for the benefit of a specific end-client, the framework gives a capacity to the Gmail administration to introduce an "end-client authorization ticket" as a component of the RPC. This ticket demonstrates that the Gmail administration is right now adjusting a solicitation for that specific end-client, this empowers the Contacts administration to actualize a protect where it just returns information for the end-client named in the ticket.

The foundation gives a focal client character administration which issues these "end-client consent tickets." An end-client login is checked by the focal personality administration, which at that point gives a client qualification, for example, a treat or OAuth token, to the client's customer gadget. Each ensuing solicitation from the customer gadget into Google needs to introduce that client accreditation.

When a service generates an end-user credential, it passes the credential to the central identity service for verification. If the end-user credential verifies correctly, the central identity service returns a short-lived "end-user permission ticket" that can be utilized for RPCs identified with the solicitation. In our model, that administration which gets the "end-client consent ticket" would be the Gmail administration, which would pass it to the Contacts administration. Starting thereon, for any falling calls, the "end-client consent ticket" can be passed on by the calling administration to the callee as an aspect of the RPC call.

Services interact in identity and authentication process.

Administration personality and access the board: The foundation offers support character, programmed shared verification, scrambled between administration correspondence and implementation of access arrangements characterized by the administration proprietor.

Secure Data Storage

As yet in the conversation, we have portrayed how we send benefits safely. We will currently go to talk about how we execute secure data piling on the structure.

Encryption at Rest

Google's foundation gives an assortment of capacity administrations, for example, Bigtable and Spanner, and focal basic administration. Most applications at Google access physical capacity in a roundabout way using these capacity administrations. The capacity administrations can be designed to utilize keys from the essential key administration to scramble data before it is moved to physical storage capacity. This key administration upholds programmed key revolution, gives broad review logs, and coordinates with the recently referenced end-client authorization pass to interface keys to specific end clients.

Performing encryption at the application layer permits the foundation to confine itself from possible dangers at the lower levels of capacity, for example, noxious plate firmware. The establishment likewise executes extra layers of insurance. We empower equipment encryption to uphold in our hard drives and SSDs and carefully track each drives through its lifecycle. Before a decommissioned encoded capacity gadget can genuinely leave our guardianship, it is cleaned utilizing a multi-step measure that incorporates two free confirmations.

Deletion of Data

Deletion of data at Google most often start with marking specific data as "scheduled for deletion" rather than removing the data entirely, it permits us to recuperate from inadvertent cancellations, regardless of whether client started or because of a bug or cycle mistake inside. In the wake of having been set apart as "planned for erasure," the information is erased following explicit assistance arrangements.

When an end-user deletes their entire account, the infrastructure notifies services that are handling end-user information that the record has been erased. The administrations would then be able to plan information related with the erased end-user account for deletion. This feature enables the developer of service to implement the end-user control quickly.

Secure Internet Communication

Until this point in this archive, we have portrayed how we secure administrations on our foundation. In this segment, we go to clarify how we guarantee correspondence between the web and these administrations.

As examined before, the framework comprises of an enormous arrangement of physical machines which are associated over the WAN or LAN and the security of administration between correspondence isn't subject to the security of the organization. In any case, we do disengage our foundation from the web into a private IP space so we can all the more effectively actualize extra assurances, for example, guards against the refusal of administration (DoS) assaults by just uncovering a subset of the machines straightforwardly to outer web traffic.

Google Front End Service

At the point when assistance needs to make itself accessible on the Internet, it can enrol itself with a foundation administration called the Google Front End (GFE). The GFE guarantees that all TLS associations are ended utilizing right testaments and following accepted procedures, for example, supporting immaculate forward mystery. The GFE furthermore applies for insurances against Denial of Service assaults (which we will talk about in more detail later). The GFE at that point advances demands for the administration utilizing the RPC security convention talked about beforehand.

As a result, any inward help which decides to distribute itself remotely utilizes the GFE as a savvy invert intermediary front end. This front end gives public IP facilitating of its public DNS name, Denial of Service (DoS) security, and TLS end. Note that GFEs run on the foundation like some other assistance and along these lines can scale to coordinate approaching solicitation volumes.

Refusal of Service (DoS) Protection

The sheer size of our foundation empowers Google to retain numerous DoS assaults essentially. We have multi-level, multi-layer DoS securities that further decrease the danger of any DoS sways on assistance running behind a GFE.

After their spine conveys an outer association with one of our server farms, it goes through a few layers of equipment and programming load-adjusting. These heap balancers report data about approaching traffic to a focal DoS administration running on the foundation. At the point when the focal DoS administration distinguishes that a DoS assault is occurring, it can design the heap balancers to drop or choke traffic related to the assault.

At the following layer, the GFE occurrences likewise report data about solicitations that they are getting to the focal DoS administration, including application layer data that the heap balancers don't have. The focal DoS administration can then additionally arrange the GFE examples to drop or choke assault traffic.

Client Authentication

After DoS security, the following stage of protection originates from our focal character administration. This administration ordinarily shows to end clients as the Google login page. Past requesting a straightforward username and secret key, the administration likewise shrewdly challenges clients for extra data dependent on hazard factors, for example, regardless of whether they have signed in from a similar gadget or a comparable area previously. In the wake of validating the client, the personality administration issues qualifications, for example, treats and OAuth tokens that can be utilized for resulting calls.

Clients likewise have the alternative of utilizing second factors, for example, OTPs or phishing-safe Security Keys when marking in. To guarantee that the advantages go past Google, they have worked in the FIDO Alliance with various gadget sellers to build up the Universal Second Factor (U2F) open norm. These gadgets are currently accessible in the market, and other essential web benefits additionally have followed Google in executing U2F uphold.

Operational Security

As yet, we have depicted how security is planned into our foundation and have likewise portrayed a portion of the instruments for secure activity, for example, access controls on RPCs.

They turn to describe how Google operates the infrastructure securely: they create infrastructure software securely, we protect our employees' machines and credentials, and they guard against dangers to the infrastructure from the two insiders and outer elements.

Safe Software Development

Past the focal source control and two-party survey highlights depicted before, they likewise give libraries that keep engineers from presenting certain classes of security bugs. For instance, they have libraries and structures that wipe out XSS weaknesses in web applications. We likewise have mechanized devices for consequently distinguishing security bugs, including fuzzers, static examination apparatuses, and web security scanners.

As a last check, we utilize manual security surveys that go from brisk emergencies for safer highlights to the top to bottom plan and usage audits for the riskiest highlights. These surveys are directed by a group that incorporates specialists across web security, cryptography, and working framework security. The reports can also result in new security library features and new fuzzers that can then be applied to other future products.

We also run a Vulnerability Rewards Program where we pay any individual who can find and educate us regarding bugs in our foundation or applications. They have been able to pay several million dollars to people who been able to help them achieve this.

Google additionally puts a lot of exertion in discovering 0-day misuses and other security issues in all the open-source programming we use and upstreaming these issues. For instance, the OpenSSL Heartbleed bug was found at Google, and we are the biggest submitter of security bug fixes and CVEs for the Linux KVM hypervisor.

Keeping Employee Devices and Credentials Safe

We make a huge interest in shielding our representatives' gadgets and qualifications from bargain and in observing movement to find expected trade-offs or illegal insider action, this is a basic piece of google interest in guaranteeing that our framework is worked securely.

Reducing Insider Risk

We forcefully limit and effectively screen the exercises of representatives who have been conceded regulatory admittance to the framework and persistently work to kill the requirement for restricted admittance for specific errands by giving computerization that can achieve similar undertakings in a protected and controlled manner, this incorporates requiring two-party endorsements for specific activities and presenting restricted APIs that permit troubleshooting without uncovering delicate data.

Google worker admittance to end-client data can be logged through low-level foundation snares. Google's security group effectively screens access designs and examines rare occasions.

Securing Google Cloud

In this part, we feature how our public cloud framework, Google Cloud, profits by the security of the basic infrastructure. In this part, we will take Google Compute Engine as illustration support and portray in detail the administration explicit security upgrades that we expand on the head of the framework.

PC Engine empowers clients to run their virtual machines on Google's framework. The Compute Engine execution comprises of a few sensible parts, most outstandingly the administration control plane and the virtual machines themselves.

The administration control plane uncovered the outer API surface and arranged undertakings like virtual machine creation and movement. It runs as an assortment of administrations on the foundation. In this way, it naturally gets central uprightness highlights, for example, a safe boot chain. The individual administrations run under detailed inside assistance accounts with the goal that each help can be conceded just the authorizations it requires when settling on distant methodology decisions (RPCs) to the remainder of the control plane. As examined before, the code for these administrations is put away in the focal Google source code store, and there is a review trail between this code and the pairs that are inevitably sent.

End-client confirmation to the Compute Engine control plane API is done through Google's concentrated personality administration, which gives security highlights, for example, capturing identification. Approval is finished utilizing the focal Identity and Access Management administration.

The organization traffic for the control plane, both from the GFEs to the main help behind it and between other control plane administrations is consequently confirmed by the framework and scrambled at whatever point it goes starting with one server farm then onto the next. Moreover, the framework has been designed to run a portion of the control plane traffic inside the server farm too.

Process Engine constant circles are encoded very still utilizing keys ensured by the focal framework key administration framework. It takes into account the robotized revolution and focal inspecting of admittance to these keys.

Clients today have the decision of whether to send traffic from their VMs to different VMs or the web free or to execute any encryption they decide for this traffic. We have begun turning out programmed encryption for the WAN crossing bounce of client VM to VM traffic. As portrayed before, all control plane WAN traffic inside the framework is as of now scrambled. Later on, we intend to exploit the equipment quickened network encryption examined before additionally to encode between VM LAN traffic inside the server farm.

The detachment gave to the VMs depends on equipment virtualization utilizing the open-source KVM stack. We have additionally solidified our specific usage of KVM by moving a portion of the control and equipment copying stack into an unprivileged cycle outside the part. We have additionally widely tried the centre of KVM utilizing methods like fluffing, static examination, and manual code audit. As referenced before, most of the ongoing freely uncovered weaknesses which have been upstreamed into KVM originated from Google.

Finally, google operational security controls are an essential part of making sure that accesses to data follow our policies. As part of Google Cloud, Compute Engine's use of customer data supports Google Cloud's use of customer data policy, namely that Google will not access or use customer data, except as necessary to provide services to customers.

CHAPTER EIGHT- HOW TO ENSURE SOLUTION AND OPERATION RELIABILITY OF CLOUD ARCHITECTURE

Introduction To The Reliability Of Cloud Architecture

The information has a very serious role to play in the understanding of reliability. Without the right information, achieving the aim of security in cloud architecture would be a far-fetched dream. In reality, no system, plan, strategy or application can be 100 per cent efficient, there's is always be something lacking. If there were a 100 per cent efficient system, there would be the need to discuss this. In every system, certain precautions must be taken to guarantee certain things. Specific steps must be observed. And so, in the case of Cloud architecture, the same principle applies.

Reliability comes into play in the place of inefficiency. When looking out for an excellent system to work with, do we check and base solely on its efficiency? It would be wrong because the system could be "100 per cent efficient" ideally speaking, but no accurate test for reliability can keep it working. Security, therefore, is agreeably vital in anything we work towards and should be applied in this line of action.

On this note, for reliability to stand out, there must be specific parameters that must be met through series of tests, that could as well correlate with past data to keep the solution and operation of a cloud architecture reliable and worthwhile to be used. It is important to note that ensuring the reliability of an application, platform, or cloud architecture will make other features they have evidence to the users.

Before we proceed in exploring the methodology behind ensuring the solution and reliability of cloud architecture, let us examine what the word "reliable" and "reliability" means. According to the Merriam Webster dictionary, we have the following definitions for Reliable:

* Able to be trusted to do or give what is required; ready to be depended on; ready to be believed; likely to be accurate or correct

* Suitable or fit to be relied on- dependable.

* Giving the same result on successive trials

While RELIABILITY means: the quality or state of being reliable; the degree to which a trial, test, or estimating strategy yields similar outcomes on repeated trials.

From the definitions above, it should be noted that reliability speaks of continuous and progressive development. It is something that lives on with time. Hence, whatever measures one must employ to ensure security has to have a continuity effect. As this is the aim of this section, there is an outlined guide for processes that will help achieve reliability goals.

Some key factors to consider while ensuring the reliability of cloud architecture (application or platform) are;

1. Operational techniques involved in running the cloud architecture must require very little manual work and mental load from the operators or users, while at the same time ensuring rapid reduction of the failures accompanying it.

2. Measurable goals considered to be reliable must be set in place, and corrections to deviation from such goals or parameters must be promptly done. This is a pivotal aspect of achieving one's reliability goals. It is therefore desirable that if you must be successful at gaining reliability, you must have to set realistic goals.

3. Flexibility, scalability, availability, and automated change management are to be considered in cloud architecture.

4. Self-healing and observance must be part of the cloud architecture.

Identifier For Cloud Architecture Reliability

In the exploration of the meaning of reliability and its relationship to cloud architecture, there is a necessity to identify the factors that must be considered in the process of achieving security of cloud architecture. These factors are very crucial and should not be taken likely.

These are treated as follows;

1. The User defines Reliability. this deals with the question "what does the user of the cloud architecture consider as reliable?" Now depending on the system your cloud architecture adopts, there are various ways to gather this data, compile it and work with it. In the case of a user-facing workload, measuring the user experience of primary importance, an example is a query success ratio. Many system workloads have different methods of getting the user-defined reliability values needed to determine what could make the cloud architecture designed reliable.

Sufficient Reliability. It is necessary to set Service Level Objectives (SLOs) that will give a reliability threshold and will also use error budgets to manage the rate of change to the cloud architecture. The cloud architecture would thus be reliable but not too secure that it becomes unjustified. Therefore, your SLOs or reliability parameters should be within a range of values

Redundancy. No single points of failure are features of a cloud architecture with high-reliability needs. Resources for reliable cloud architecture are replicated across multiple failure domains. Failure domains are pools of resources that are capable of failing independently.

Horizontal Scalability. Traffic growth or data growth through the addition of more resources should be accommodated in your cloud architecture, and it is essential to include this factor.

Overload Tolerance: This is self-explanatory. In case of an overload to the cloud architecture, a useful tolerance feature is essential to avoid crashing of the cloud.

Rollback Capacity. Change is constant and is essential to ensure growth and development of the cloud architecture. However, a method to undo a modification done to the cloud architecture is highly relevant – that is, roll back the difference.

Traffic Control. Countless clients sending traffic to cloud architecture at the same instant can lead to cascading failures as a result of traffic spikes, to control this, it is essential not to synchronize requests across clients.

Test Failure Recovery. Failure recovery is an important feature, but it is essential to test it periodically. If it is not tested, it may not function when you need it. Set failure recovery procedures and test them out regularly. Some methods to test include rolling back a release and restoring data from backups.

Failure Detection. In case of failures in the cloud architecture, a method to detect these failures right on time should be put in place.

Alerting too soon and too late is not right, to prevent these, the delay before notification must be set the right possible way.

Incremental Changes. Changes made to the cloud architecture should be done gradually with "canary testing" to detect bugs in the early stages where their impact to users is minimal. Instantaneous global changes are hazardous.

Coordinated Emergency Response. Operational practices that minimize the duration of outages, as well as consider the customer's experience and users well-being should be observed. Hence, advanced formalization of response procedures with well-defined roles and communication channels.

System Observability Feature. The cloud architecture system should be sufficiently developed to enable rapid triaging, troubleshooting, and diagnosis of a problem to minimize outages.

Capacity Management. The cloud architecture should be equipped with the function to give traffic and provision resources in advance of peak traffic events.

Documentation and Automated Emergency Responses. Pre-plan emergency actions, document them and ideally automate and corporate them into the cloud architecture in case of emergencies. People find it difficult in defining what should be done in such situations.

Toil Reduction. "What is toil?" one may ask. Toil is repetitive manual work with no enduring value. It is important to note that toil increases with service growth. Reduction of total elimination of drudgery in the cloud architecture is one of the things to seek out for; otherwise, operational work would become too much for the users, thus leaving little or no room for the successful growth of the cloud architecture.

We have gone a long way to identify factors and markers that can make cloud architecture reliable. The knowledge of these factors is on one ground, but applying this knowledge in the best way to ensure reliability is another ball game altogether. It is essential to know how to use this knowledge to achieve a successful and reliable cloud architecture since cloud architecture is a significant and crucial component of the currently fast-developing world we live in today.

Ensuring Solution And Operational Reliability Of Cloud Architecture

These are a series of steps or practices as you may like to call them, that must be followed for proper functioning and reliability of cloud architecture. These include;

Reliability Goal Definition. Existing customer experience, tolerance for errors and mistakes should be accounted for while defining reliability goals. If the data that a user expects from a cloud architecture is not there, then the overall uptime goal of 100 per cent over an infinite amount of time is both meaningless and will not be achieved.

On this note, SLOs based on the user experience should be set; this is carried out successfully by measuring the reliability metrics as close to the user as possible. Estimating dependability at the worker ought to be the final retreat for this cycle. A high SLO that makes the user happy is ideal and no higher than that.

A target lower than 100 per cent for uptime and other vital metrics is strongly advised, although target should be close to 100 per cent. This target allows for fast and quality service.

Reliability goals that are achievable and set according to the customer experience help determine the highest pace and scope of changes that users can tolerate.

Competitive benchmark analysis could be used if existing customer experiences can not be measured. Measure customer experience even if you cannot define goals yet, in case of absence of comparable competition.

SLIs, SLOs and SLAs. Service Level Indicators (SLIs) are quantitative measures of some aspect of the provided level of service. It is a metric and not a target. Service Level Objectives (SLOs) are the targets for the reliability of your cloud architecture. SLOs are very vital in making data-driven decisions about safety; thus, they are the core of SRE practices. SLOs are the values for SLIs, and cloud architecture is considered reliable if the SLIs are at or above this value. Service Level Agreements (SLAs) are contracts with the user, which includes consequences of meeting or missing the stated SLOs; they can be explicit or implicit. It is an excellent practice to have stricter internal SLOs than external SLAs.

Error budgeting helps to manage development velocity of the cloud architecture. Launch new features quickly if the error budget is not yet consumed. However, freeze or slow down changes if the error budget is close to zero, then invest engineering resources into reliability features.

Examples of SLIs

For serving systems, the following are typical SLIs and very important, hence ensure you go through them critically and carefully, to milk the juice therein:

Availability: There's always the question of how possible it is to tell precisely how much fraction of time is required per time in any service; this is where availability comes in to play. One may also ask, "How can I identify this?" this is also covered here. More often than not, this factor is determined and recognized following well-formed requests that succeed—for example, 99% seals the deal.

Latency: Then again, on the off chance that you have ever had concerns on how much time a certain percentage of request could take to be fulfilled, welcome to LATENCY. It is often defined in terms of percentile other than 50th—for example, 99th percentile at 300 ms.

Quality: At this juncture, you may want to know how much response a specific service has garnered. If this is the case, Quality tells you how good a particular response is. Quality is often defined in terms of specific services, showing the degree to which the substance of the reaction to a solicitation fluctuates from the ideal reaction content. Quality here can be two distinct folds (awful or great) or even better, and we can assess quality between the scope of 0% to 100%.

For information handling frameworks, the accompanying SLIs are ordinary and similarly pertinent:

Coverage: In a case where you are concerned with the amount of data that has been processed, Coverage tells you the fraction of data that has been processed—for example, 99.9% and so on.

Correctness: For you to be able to determine the responses that are bound to be correct and acceptable, correctness addresses that for you— for example, 99.99%.

Freshness: tells you how latest the data source is, or how much of aggregated responses you have present in your system, the more frequent, the better—for example, 20 minutes.

Throughput: to find out how much data is going through processing, you welcome to Throughput. Therein lies your solution. Thus, Throughput measures the amount of data being processed per time for a model, 500 MiB/sec or 1000 Rps.

The following SLIs are common for storage systems:

Durability: As an operator, many cases may arise for you to retrieve data written in the system for future purposes - this is where durability comes in. Durability, therefore, helps you determine your capabilities to access saved write-ups on the system for future uses. Thus, when any data is lost or misplaced from the system, it spells room for your durability metric—for instance, 99.9999%.

Throughput: Throughput tells you how much data is being processed per time.

Latency: Latency talks about the duration used for any request to be fulfilled. It speaks loudly about time measurement.

Incorporate Observability into the Cloud Architecture; this would include monitoring, tracking, logging, debugging, profiling and other methods involved in observing, and this is to ensure the cloud architecture maximizes observability to the fullest. A well-designed cloud architecture strives to have the necessary observability starting with the development phase. Common anti-patterns to avoid are over-engineering monitoring and over-alerting, and this can be achieved by actively deleting time series, dashboards, and alerts not looked at or rarely fired during the initial launch stages.

Design for Scale and high availability. Your cloud architecture needs to be very scalable and readily available. A multi-region architecture with failover should be designed into your cloud architecture if you want it to be available even when an entire region is down. Get rid of single points of failure like a single-region master database as it can cause a global outrage if unreachable. Also, by identifying architecture components that can not grow beyond the resource limits of a single zone and redesigning these components to be horizontally scalable, since such elements have hard cutoff points on their versatility and frequently require manual reconfiguration to carry outgrowth, you can eliminate scalability bottlenecks. An alternative to redesigning is replacing these components with managed services designed to scale with no user action.

Cloud engineering ought to be planned in such a manner that it would detect overload and return quality responses to the user or partially give traffic rather than failing. Implementing exponential backoff with jitter in your cloud architecture can prevent a generation of instantaneous traffic spikes from large groups of users since these spikes can potentially crash the cloud architecture. However, if the cloud architecture experiences known periods of peak traffic, make sure to prepare for such events adequately to avoid significant loss of revenue and traffic. Finally, do not wait for disasters to strike; periodically test as well as verify your disaster recovery procedures and processes you have put in place in your cloud architecture.

Build-in Flexible and Automated Deployment Capabilities. Redesign the cloud architecture to support rollback and test the rollback processes periodically, if there is no defined way to undo specific changes. Spreading out traffic for time promotions (this includes special events) and launches helps to significantly prevent instantaneous traffic spikes that could crash your cloud architecture at the scheduled start time. Canary system testing alerts one to problems and might even automatically halt rollouts, therefore it is beneficial to implement progressive implementation with canary testing.

Automation is functional and an enormous arsenal added to the design of your cloud architecture, but, it is not a cure, this is because since it accompanies a decent amount of support expenses and dangers to dependability past its underlying turn of events and arrangement costs. Hence, a continuous process of inventorying and assessing the cost of toil on the team managing the cloud architecture is much recommended before investing in customized automation.

Efficient Alerting System should be Used. Optimize alerting delay by tuning the configured delay before the monitoring system notifies humans of a problem to minimize outages while maximizing signal versus noise. Set to trigger alerts based on the direct impact on user experiences, which is based on symptoms and not causes.

A Collaborative Incident Management Process Should be built. Failing to meet SLOs is inevitable for any cloud architecture. However, in the absence of an SLO, your customers will still define based on their experience what the acceptable service level is, this will escalate to your technical support or similar group irrespective of the contents of your SLA, to satisfy your users adequately, it is recommended that you establish and regularly implement an incident management plan.

Let us take a few examples of the Incident Management Plan. This part is one of the "bumpy rides" you may encounter; this is where we would draw the curtain in this one.

Example Of Incident Management Plan

* Should I delegate in any case? Indeed, if you and your group can't resolve this.

* Production issues have been recognized (caution, page) or heightened to me.

* Should I include more individuals? Indeed, if it is affecting over X% of clients or if it takes more than Y minutes to determine. If all else fails, consistently include more individuals, particularly during business hours.

* Attend repeating after death occurrence survey meeting to talk about and staff things to do.

* Is this a crisis or are SLO(s) in danger? If all else fails, treat it as a

crisis

* Define when the occurrence is finished, this may require affirmation from a Support delegate.

* Define a virtual correspondences channel—for instance, IRC, Hangouts Chat, or Slack.

* Define a primary communications channel—for example, IRC, Hangouts Chat, or Slack.

CHAPTER NINE- EXAM GUIDE

Do you want to be a certified Google cloud professional architect or validate your skills to work on cloud innovations and technologies? Professional Google Cloud certified test is the appropriate answer. Google cloud architect certification exam is geared towards having significant knowledge of working on Google Cloud. The Google Cloud Certified Professional Cloud Architect Exam Guide is an essential resource for anyone preparing for this highly sought-after, professional-level certification. Proficient level affirmation. Nitty-gritty clarifications of vital subjects incorporate dissecting and characterizing specialized and business measures, movement arranging, planning and building storage frameworks, organizations, and process analysis.

Offering types of assistance appropriate for a wide scope of uses, especially in high-development territories of examination and AI, Google Cloud is quickly picking up a piece of the overall industry in the distributed computing world. Associations are looking for guaranteed IT experts with the capacity to convey and work for framework, administrations, and organizations in the Google Cloud. Take your profession a notch higher approving your abilities and winning accreditation. The Google Cloud Certified Professional Cloud Architect Exam Guide is a must-have for IT professionals preparing for certification to deploy and manage Google cloud services

Overview Of Google Cloud Architect Exam

Google Professional Cloud Architect Exam enables individuals and organizations to have the technical knowledge and analytical skills to leverage Google Cloud technologies. With proper knowledge and understanding of the Google cloud and cloud architecture, the organization or individuals involved can, develop designs, manage, secure available and dynamic solutions to set any business objectives in motion. A certified Cloud Architect is an individual who has proficiency in all the aspects of solution design, enterprise cloud strategy and best architectural practices. The certified Cloud Architect should also be able to show a high level of experience with software development methodology and multi-tiered distributed applications which span hybrid or multi-cloud environments. The Professional Cloud Architect exam was set up to assess, to test knowledge of the ability of an individual to plan a cloud solution architecture, manage the cloud solution infrastructure, design (for compliance and security), analyze technical processes, optimize business processes, ensure operations reliability and manage the implementation of cloud architecture.

It is imperative that the exam structure and format be understood before attempting the exam; this is an overview of the Google Cloud Architect Certification exam.

Google cloud architecture is not limited to any range of roles yet, and it is mainly intended for

- Enterprise/solutions architect
- Operations team(members of the operations team)
- Graduates who might want to assemble a vocation as cloud planners
- System administrators

When preparing for Google Cloud Architect exam, you must make sure you understand the objectives. Google made it easy to understand by dividing the exam syllabus into various subject areas. Below are the topics that are covered during the exam; this should be your focus during the preparation.

1. Plan and Design a Cloud Solution Architecture
Design a solution infrastructure that business requirements

Design a solution infrastructure meeting technical requirements

Design storage, network, and compute resources

Create a migration plan

Envision of the solution improvements for future

2. Provision and Management of Solution Infrastructure
The configuration of network topologies

The configuration of individual storage systems

The configuration of computer systems

3. Compliance and Security Design
Design Security

Design legal compliance

4. Analyze and Optimize business and specialized processes
Analyze and characterized the specialized process

Investigate and characterize business Processes

Create a methodology for testing arrangement versatility under creation

5. Implementation Management

Prompt activity/improvement and guarantee that arrangement is executed effectively

Write and read the languages for application development

6. Ensure the reliability of solution and operations

Log, monitor, and alert solution

Release management and deployment

Support troubleshooting of operations

Evaluate different measures for quality control

1. DESIGNING AND PLANNING A CLOUD SOLUTION ARCHITECTURE

To design a solution infrastructure that will meet the requirements of a business, you must consider the following facts:

- Possible cases of business use and the product strategy
- Possible ways of optimizing cost
- Support for the design
- Integration with multi-cloud environments (external systems)
- Movement of data
- Design decision trade-offs
- But, build or modify
- Measurement of success – e.g. key performance indicators

- Observability and compliance

Consider the following facts when designing a solution that should meet technical requirements

- Failover design and high availability
- Cloud resources elasticity
- Ability of the design to be produced in a range of capabilities (ability to meet growth requirements)
- Latency and performance

For designing compute resources, storage and network, consider the following:

- Integration with multi-cloud environments and systems in the premises of the organization (on-premises systems)
- Cloud-native networking
- Choosing data process technologies
- Choosing appropriate storage types
- Choosing compute resources
- Matching the compute needs to the platform products

Consider the following facts when creating a migration plan

- Integrating solutions with already existing systems
- Migrating data and systems to support the solution
- Mapping licencing

- Network planning
- Testing and proof of concept
- Dependency management planning

For envisioning future solution improvements, the following facts should be considered:

- Technology and cloud improvement
- Business evolution
- Advocacy and publicity

2. MANAGING AND PROVIDING A SOLUTION INFRASTRUCTURE

When configuring network topologies, the following should be considered:

- Hybrid networking (extending to systems within the premises of the organization)
- Extending to systems outside the premises of the organization that may include GCP to GCP communication
- Data protection and security

For individual storage system configuration, consider the following:

- Allocation of data storage
- Compute provisioning/data processing
- Access and security management
- Configuration of the network for late cy and data transfer

- Data life cycle management and data retention
- Data growth management

For compute systems, the following should be considered:

- Compute system provisioning
- Configuration of computing volatility
- Configuration of a network for compute nodes
- Configuration of infrastructure provisioning technology, e.g. terraform/deployment manager
- Use of Kubernetes for container orchestration

3. DESIGNING FOR SECURITY ANC COMPLIANCE

Consider the following when designing for security

- IAM – identity and access management
- Resource hierarchy – organizations, folders, projects
- Data security – encryption
- Testing of penetration
- SoD – separation of duties
- Managed encryption keys with cloud KMS – managing customer

Consider these facts when designing for compliance

- Certification of industry
- Audits

- Legislation – data privacy, health record privacy
- Commercial – handling of sensitive data such as credit card information

4. ANALYZING AND OPTIMIZING TECHNICAL AND BUSINESS PROCESSES

Consider the following when analyzing and defining technical processes:

- Life cycle plan of software development
- Continuous deployment/continuous integration
- Post mortem analysis culture (troubleshooting)
- Validation and testing
- Provisioning and service catalogue
- Disaster recovery and business continuity

Consider the following when analyzing and defining business processes:

- Stakeholder management – facilitation and influencing
- Management change
- Skills readiness/team assessment
- Process of decision making
- Management of customer success
- Resource optimization/cost optimization

You should also be able to develop procedures that ensure the resilience of a solution in production

5. MANAGING IMPLEMENTATION

When advising development/operation team to ensure the successful deployment of the solution, consider the following factors:

- API best practices
- Development of application
- Framework testing –integration/unit/load
- System migrating and data tooling

When interacting with Google Cloud using GCP SDK, Consider the following

- Google cloud shell
- Local installation

You must also ensure the reliability of the solution and operations. You can do this by:

- Monitoring/logging/profiling/alerting solution
- Release and deployment management
- Assisting in solution support during operations
- Evaluation of quality control measure

During the Cloud Architect certification exam, some questions may refer you to case studies that describe a fictitious business and solution. These case studies provide additional context that will help you choose your answers. One such case study is:

TerramEarth

It is one of the sample case studies that can be used during the Professional Cloud Architect exam. This case study describes a fictitious business and solution concept, and this helps to provide additional context to the exam questions.

TerramEarth is an industry that manufactures heavy equipment for the agricultural and mining sectors. 20% of their business is from agriculture, and 80% is from mining. They have over 600 service centres and dealers in 100 countries with the mission to build products that will aid their customers to become more productive.

1. SOLUTION CONCEPT

TerramEarthhas 20 million vehicles in operation that gather collect 120 fields of data every second. Data for analysis can be assessed when any of these vehicles have been serviced because data is stored locally on the vehicle. This data is downloaded by a maintenance port which can be used to adjust operational parameters, and this allows the vehicles to be upgraded in the field with new computing modules.TerramEarth can collect data directly from a cellular network which has approximately 200,000 vehicles connected to it. TerramEarth, therefore, collects 9TB per day from these connected vehicles, this is done at a rate of 120 fields every second, with daily operations of 22 hours.

2. EXISTING TECHNICAL ENVIRONMENT

TerramEarth has an existing architecture that is composed of Linux and Windows-based systems that all reside in a U.S west-coast-based data centre. These systems upload files gotten from the field (CSV files) via FTP and store the data in their data warehouse. Aggregated reports are always based on data that is three weeks old because this process takes a lot of time. TerramEarth can preemptively stock replacement parts, spare parts and reduces planned downtime of their work vehicles with the data that is stored in their data warehouse. While they wait for replacement parts, some customers stay without their vehicles for about three to four weeks because the data is stale.

3. BUSINESS REQUIREMENTS

TerramEarth should have the ability to partner with different companies to create a compelling offering for their customers (e.g. seed and fertilizer suppliers in the agricultural business)

They should be able to have and support dealer network with a lot more data on how their customers use their equipment to better position new products and services

They should be able to decrease the downtime of vehicles to less than one week.

4. TECHNICAL REQUIREMENTS

Improvement of data in their data warehouse

Increase the security of transfer of data from the equipment to the data centre

Ability to use equipment and customer data to predict customer needs

Ability to create a backup strategy

Expansion beyond a single data centre

5. APPLICATION 1: DATA INGESTION

Here a Python application reads the uploaded files gotten from a single server and writes to their data warehouse

Compute:

Windows Server 2008 R2

16 CPUs

128GB of RAM

10 TB of local HDD storage

6. APPLICATION 2: REPORTING

It is an application (off the shelf) that is used by business analysts to run a daily check to see the equipment that needs repair. This application is limited to two analysts at a time.

Compute

Application. License tied to the number of physical CPUs

Windows Server 2008 R2

16 CPUs

32 GB RAM

500 GB HDD

Data warehouse

A single PostgreSQL server

RedHat Linux

64 CPUs

128 GB RAM

4x 6TB HDD in RAID O

7. EXECUTIVE STATEMENT

Our unique ability to build better vehicles for lower costs than our competitors has always been our competitive advantage in our manufacturing process. Even though I'm concerned that we lack the skills to undergo the next of transformations in our industry, new products with different approaches and styles are continually being developed. While addressing an immediate market need through incremental innovations, our goals are to build more skills which will help us harness the new waves of transformation.

Other examples of fictitious case studies are Mountkirk Games and Dress4win

MOUNTKIRK GAMES

Mountkirk Games makes online, multiplayer, session-based games for mobile platforms. All their games are built using integrated server-side. Historically, physical servers have been leased by cloud providers. They have had to face problems such as scaling their global audience, application servers, MySQL databases, and analytics tools, due to the unexpected popularity of some of their games.

To be able to scale their problems is to writing game statistics to files and sending them through an ETL tool that loads them unto a centralized MySQL database for reporting is their current model.

1. Solution concept

Mountkirk Games is building another game, which they hope to be well known to be able to capture streaming metrics, carry out intensive analytics and also take advantage of its auto-scaling server environment and integrate with a managed NoSQL database they plan to deploy the game's backend on Compute Engine

2. Business requirements

Increase to a global footprint

Reduce latency to all customers

Improve uptime because downtime is the loss of players

Increase the efficiency of the cloud resources used

3. TECHNICAL REQUIREMENTS

Requirements for game backend platform

Based on game activity, dynamically scale up or down

Associate with a conditional information base support of overseeing client profiles and game state

Storage of game activity in a time series database service for future analysis

Ensure that the information is not lost due to processing issues as the system scales

Run hardened Linux distro

Requirements for game analytics platform

Dynamically, either scale up or down based on the activity of the game

Cycle approaching information on the fly legitimately from the server of the game.

Data that arrives late due to slow mobile networks is processed

Permit inquiries about accessing at any rate 10 TB of authentic information

Cycle documents that are regularly transferred by clients' cell phones

4. EXECUTIVE STATEMENT

Our last successful game had low user adoption, and this affected the game's reputation because it did not scale well with our previous cloud provider. To assess the speed and soundness of the game, just as different measurements that give a more in-depth insight into usage patterns so we can adapt the game to target users, our investors want more key performance indicators (KPIs). Additionally, we want to replace MySQL and move to an environment that provides auto-scaling and low latency load balancing and frees us up from managing physical servers because our current technology stack cannot provide the scale we need.

DRESS4WIN

Dress4Win is a web-based company that helps its users manage and organize their wardrobe using a web app and mobile application. They adapt their administrations through publicizing, internet business, referrals, and a freemium application model. The organization likewise develops a functioning informal community that associates its clients with planners and retailers. The application has developed from a couple of workers in the organizer's carport to a few hundred workers and apparatuses in an arranged server farm. Be that as it may, due to the expansion in clients, their foundation limit is presently deficient. Dress4Win is focusing on a full movement to a public cloud because of its quick development and the organization's longing to improve quicker

1. SOLUTION CONCEPT

Dress4Win is moving their turn of events and test situations for the first phase of their migration to the cloud. Because of their current infrastructure at a single location, they are also building a disaster recovery site. Not sure which components of their architecture they can migrate as is and which elements they need to change before relocating them.

2. EXISTING TECHNICAL ENVIRONMENT

As earlier stated, the Dress4Win application is served out of a single data centre area. Ubuntu LTS v16.04 is where all servers run.

The Databases:

MySQL. One worker for client information, stock, static information,

128 GB of RAM

MySQL 5.7

2x 5 TB HDD (RAID 1)

8 core CPUs

Computing:

40 web application servers providing micro-services static content and based APIs

Nginx

Tomcat – Java

32 GB of RAM

Four core CPUs

Data analysis

20 Apache Hadoop/Spark servers:

Eight core CPUs

128 GB of RAM

Real-time trending calculations

HDD 4x 5 TB (RAID 1)

About three RabbitMQ servers for messaging, social notifications, and events:

32GB of RAM

Eight core CPUs

Different servers:

Jenkins, monitoring, bastion hosts, security scanners

Eight core CPUs

32GB of RAM

Storage appliances:

iSCSI for VM hosts
Fibre channel SAN – MySQL databases

1 PB total storage; 400 TB available

NAS – image storage, logs, backups

100 TB total storage; 35 TB available

3. BUSINESS REQUIREMENT

The building of a reproducible and reliable environment with scaled parity of production.

Holding fast to a lot of security and personality, access the board best practices to improve security

Improve business agility and speed of advancement through fast provisioning of new assets

Break down and upgrade engineering for better execution in the cloud

4. TECHNICAL REQUIREMENTS

Easily create non-production environments in the cloud

Provisioning resources in the cloud by the implementation of an automation framework

Deploying applications to the on-premises data cloud or centre by the implementation of a continuous deployment process

Backing failover of the creation condition to cloud during a crisis

Scramble information on the wire and very still

Backing various private associations between the creation of server farm and cloud condition.

5. EXECUTIVE STATEMENT

Our investors are concerned that a competitor could use a public cloud platform to offset their up-front investment and free them so that they can focus on the development of better features. They are also concerned about our ability to contain costs and scale with our current infrastructure. 80% of our capacity is sitting idle while at other times our traffic patterns are highest in the mornings and weekend evenings.

Our capital consumption is currently surpassing our quarterly projections. Relocating to the cloud will probably cause an underlying increment in spending; however, we hope to change before our next equipment invigorates cycle completely. Our all-out expense of possession (TCO) examination throughout the following five years for a public cloud procedure accomplishes a cost decrease somewhere in the range of 30% and a half over our present model.

SUMMARY

The Google Cloud Professional Architect exam covers a lot of broad areas including the

- Planning of cloud solutions
- Managing of cloud solutions
- The Securing of systems and process
- Complying with industry and government regulations and rules
- Maintenance of solutions deployed for production and monitoring of the application
- Understanding of technical and business requirements and considerations

All these areas require both business and technical skills. For example, Architects need to understand issues such as accelerating the pace of development, maintaining and reporting on the service-level agreement, reducing operational expenses and assisting with regulatory compliance, since they regularly work with non-technical colleagues. In the realm of technical knowledge, architects are expected to understand functional requirements around computing, storage and networking as well as non-functional requirements of service such as availability and scalability. Some exam questions reference the case studies.

CHAPTER TEN - PROFESSIONAL CLOUD ARCHITECT EXAM

The Professional Cloud Architect practice exam will help familiarize you with the types of questions you will encounter during the certification exam. It will also help you tell your level of readiness and inform you if there will be a need for more preparation and practical experience.

The successful completion of this practice exam does not in any way guarantee that you will pass the certification exam. Reasons being that the actual exam takes longer time and covers a broader range of topics. You are advised to refer to the exam guide for a list of topics you could use for a test.

* A company was planning to migrate their on-premises Microsoft SQL server to Google Cloud with minimal efforts. They want to set up a high availability solution across zones. How do you set up the high accessibility for the information base?

A. Move the Microsoft SQL Server to Cloud Spanner, as it is circulated universally

B. Make a Read Replica for the Microsoft SQL Server and arrange its failover.

C. Use Windows Clustering Server Failover and the SQL Server always-on availability groups

D. Move to Cloud SQL and empower programmed failover

* An organization is intending to have its basic application on Google Cloud. It needs to guarantee that the application will deal with the heap regardless of whether a whole zone falls flat. What two alternatives would you suggest?

A. Try not to choose the "Multi-zone" alternative while making you oversaw occasion gathering.

B. Spread your oversaw occasion bunch more than two zones and overprovision by 100%. (for Two Zone)

C. Make a local unmanaged occasion gathering and spread your occurrences over numerous zones.

D. Overprovision your provincial oversaw occurrence bunch by in any event half. (for Three Zones)

* A Company is arranging the relocation of their web application to Google App Engine. Be that as it may, they would keep on utilizing their on-premises information base. How might they set up application?

A. Arrangement the application utilizing App Engine Standard condition with Cloud VPN to associate with the information base

B. Arrangement the application utilizing App Engine Flexible condition with Cloud VPN to associate with an information base

C. Arrangement the application utilizing App Engine Standard condition with Cloud Router to associate with an information base

D. Arrangement the application utilizing App Engine Flexible condition with Cloud Router to associate with d

* An organization is relocating its information to Google Cloud utilizing Cloud VPN burrow. They are attempting to set up Virtual Private Network on Cloud Which of the accompanying conditions is genuine concerning the IPs?

A. Essential IPs between on-premises and Cloud ought not to cover, while Secondary IPs can cover

B. Essential and Secondary IPs between on-premises and Cloud can cover

C. Essential IPs between on-premises and Cloud can cover, while Secondary IPs ought not to cover

D. Essential and Secondary IPs between on-premises and Cloud ought not to cover

* An organization is facilitating its web facilitating stage on Google Cloud utilizing Google Kubernetes Engine. The application now needs to credit instalments and should be PCI-DSS agreeable. By what method can the organization handle the necessity?

A. As GCP is PCI-DSS objection, there is no different taking care of for singular administrations

B. GKE isn't PCI-DSS agreeable as administrations run on shared hosts, and the necessity can't be satisfied

C. GKE and GCP gives you instruments to deal with PCI-DSS consistency

D. GKE is PCI-DSS protest, and no extra changes are

* An organization has its applications on Google Cloud. They handle PII information and need to ensure PII touchy information like email, address, telephone number, Mastercard before the information is put away on their framework for examination. By what means should the organization handle the equivalent?

A. Perform hashing of PII information utilizing SHA256

B. De-distinguish the information utilizing Data misfortune avoidance API

C. Perform information encryption utilizing cyclic encryption

D. Design regex examples of dealing with all the PII information and perform redaction.

* An organization has a lot of information sources from various frameworks utilized for announcing. Over some time, a ton of information is missing, and you are approached to perform irregularity recognition. How might you plan the framework?

A. Use Dataprep with Data Studio

B. Burden in Cloud Storage and use Dataflow with Data Studio

C. Burden in Cloud Storage and use Dataprep with Data Studio

D. Use Dataflow with Data Studio

* A customer needs to store records from one area and recover them from another area. Security prerequisites are that nobody ought to have the option to get to the substance of the document while it is facilitated in the cloud. What is the ideal choice?

A. Default encryption ought to be adequate

B. Client Supplied Encryption Keys (CSEK)

C. Client Managed Encryption Keys (CMEK)

D. Customer side encryption

* A customer is utilizing Cloud SQL information base to serve inconsistently changing query tables that have information utilized by applications. The applications won't change the tables. As they venture into other geographic districts, they need to guarantee brilliant execution. What do you suggest?

A. Migrate to Cloud Spanner

B. Read replicas

C. Instance high availability configuration

D. Migrate to Cloud Storage

* Your client is moving their stockpiling item to Google Cloud Storage (GCS). The information contains recognizable data (PII) and delicate client data. What security technique would it be a good idea for you to use for GCS?

A. Utilize marked URLs to produce time-bound admittance to objects.

B. Award IAM read-just admittance to clients, and use default ACLs on the can.

C. Award no Google Cloud Identity and Access Management (Cloud IAM) functions to clients, and utilize granular ACLs on the pail.

D. Make randomized pail and item names. Empower community, yet just give explicit document URLs to individuals who don't have Google records and need access

* Your organization needs to follow whether somebody is available in a gathering room held for a booked gathering. There are 1000 gathering grooms across five workplaces on three mainlands. Each room is furnished with a movement sensor that reports its status consistently. The information from the movement identifier incorporates just a sensor ID and a few various discrete things of data. Investigators will utilize this information, along with data about record proprietors and office areas. Which information base sort would it be advisable for you to utilize?

A. NoSQL

B. Flat file

C. Blobstore

D. Relational

CHAPTER ELEVEN - CONCLUSION

Google Cloud's Architecture Framework portrays best practices, makes usage suggestions, and expounds on items and administrations. The structure expects to assist you with planning your Google Cloud arrangement, so it best matches your business needs. Seasoned experts created the framework at Google Cloud, including customer engineers, solution architects, cloud reliability engineers, and members of the professional service organization. Creating and managing Cloud Resources is one of the recommended initial quests for the Google Cloud learner – you will come in with little or no prior cloud knowledge, and come out with a pragmatic encounter that you can apply to your first Google Cloud venture, From composing Cloud Shell orders and conveying your first virtual machine, to running applications on Kubernetes Engine or with load adjusting. This course brings you into the essential concepts and terminologies used for working with the Google Cloud Platform. It doesn't only teach you but also helps you compare many of the computing and storage facilities available in the Google Cloud Platform, and this includes Google cloud SQL, Google Kubernetes Engine, Google App Engine, Google Cloud Storage, Google Compute Engine. It will also teach you essential policy and resource management, including the Google Cloud Identity and Access Management, the Google Cloud Resource Manager Hierarchy. Amongst other courses, you'll be taught how to design and develop cloud-native applications that integrate managed services from the Google Cloud Platform. You'll be taught how to create repeatable deployments by treating infrastructure as code, choose the correct execution environment for a particular application and monitor application performance. This will be done through a progression of blends of demos, hands-on lab and introductions. You are allowed to complete labs in your favourite language/code (Java, Python or Node J's). Through a combination of hands-on lab, demos and presentations, you'll learn how to apply the best practices for application development and use of appropriate GCP storage services for storing of objects, analytics, caching and relational data(you can do all this in our preferred language: Python or Java, Nodes.js). You'll be taught how to use GCP services and pre-trained machine learning APIs to build scalable, secure and intelligent cloud-native applications.

This course teaches you how to secure and also integrate the components of your application. Through a combination of hands-on lab, demos and presentations, you'll learn how to design and develop more secure applications, implement federated identity management and integrate your application components through the use of event-driven processing, API gateways and messaging (all these you can do in your favourite language/code – this is to enable you to finish as a professional).

You are introduced to the comprehensive, flexible infrastructure and platform services provided by Google Cloud with the focus on Compute Engine. You'll explore and deploy solution elements and infrastructure components such as networks and virtual machines, application services through a combination of demos, hands-on lab and presentations. Through the console and Cloud Shell, you'll learn how to use the Google Cloud. You'll also be taught the role of a cloud architect, the different approaches to infrastructure design and the virtual networking configuration, projects, network, subnetwork, up address and firewall rules. This course also covers deploying practical solutions including securely interconnecting systems, security and access management, customer-supplied encryption keys, quotas and billing, and resource monitoring.

The courses offered will cover a broad scope of areas, including:

1. Plan and Design of a Cloud Solution Architecture
Design a solution infrastructure meeting business requirements

Design a solution infrastructure meeting technical requirements

Design storage, network, and compute resources

Create a migration plan

Envision of the solution improvements for future

2. Provision and Management of Solution Infrastructure
The configuration of network topologies

The configuration of individual storage systems

The configuration of computer systems

3. Compliance and Security Design
Design Security

Design legal compliance

4. Analysis and Optimization of business and specialized cycles
Analyze and define technical processes

Analyze and define business Processes

Develop procedures for testing solution resilience under production

5. Implementation Management

Advise operation/development and ensure that solution is implemented successfully

Read and write the languages for application development

6. Ensuring the reliability of solution and operations

Log, monitor, and alert solution

Release management and deployment

Support troubleshooting of operations

Evaluate different measures for quality control

To advance your preparation for the certification exam, we recommend you go through this material over and over again. Completing this foundational training can provide you with appropriate knowledge of Google's recommended best practices, thus bridging the technical knowledge gap. This training can improve your chance of success on the job you seek as well as certification assessment. Google certifications are an indicator of proficiency with their technology. Google Cloud certifications validate the expertise of individuals and show their ability to transform businesses with Google Cloud technology.

The Architecting with Google Kubernetes Engine specialization: This specialization, in general, will show you how to actualize arrangements utilizing Google Kubernetes Engine. In this course, Architecting with Google Kubernetes Engine, you'll learn how to build on your ability to Architect with GKE, and it includes hands-on labs for you to have a first-hand experience of its functionalities. You'll also learn how to define identity and access management roles as well as Kubernetes pod security policies. Unless you have successfully built an infrastructure for logging and monitoring, there will be no way to deliver a reliable and maintainable solution. Monitoring the application you designed will help you make decisions based on data rather than on just any impression. You'll also be introduced to use cases for a range of GCP managed storage services within Kubernetes applications. You could actualize your capacity frameworks, and that is a legitimate decision. Be that as it may, utilizing oversaw administrations can get you into creation quicker, so they merit your thought. This course teaches individuals and organizations (operations team) the following skills:

- Understanding how software containers work
- Understanding the architecture of Kubernetes
- Understanding the architecture of Google Cloud Platform
- Understanding how pod networking works in Kubernetes Engine Create and manage Kubernetes Engine clusters using the GCP Console and cloud/ kubectl commands
- Launch, roll back and expose jobs in Kubernetes
- Manage access control using Kubernetes RBAC and Google Cloud IAM
- Managing pod security policies and network policies
- Using Secrets and ConfigMaps to isolate security credentials and configuration artefacts
- Understanding GCP choices for managed storage services monitor applications running in Kubernetes Engine.

This course also covers a section of the architecture framework, which explores how operational excellence results from efficiently running, managing and monitoring systems that deliver business value. Operational greatness causes you to manufacture an establishment for another basic rule, unwavering quality.

To achieve operational excellence, use these strategies:

Mechanize manufacture, test, and send.

Utilize persistent mix and consistent sending (CI/CD) pipelines to incorporate computerized testing with your deliveries.

Perform computerized mix testing and sending.

Screen business destinations measurements.

Characterize, measure, and alarm on applicable business measurements.

Direct fiasco recuperation testing.

Try not to trust that a fiasco will strike. Rather, occasionally check that your catastrophe recuperation methods work and test the cycles normally. Some prescribed procedures educated are:

- Increase software development and release velocity.
- Monitor for system health and business health.
- Plan and design for failures.

Increment advancement and delivery speed

Utilize a CI/CD way to deal with increment speed. To begin with, you make your product improvement group more beneficial and mechanize mix testing into the construct cycle. You robotize arrangement after your construct meets your particular testing rules. Your engineers can make littler and more successive changes. The progressions are altogether tried, and an opportunity to convey them is decreased.

You can pick how your application is turned out. It's a best practice to do canary testing and watch your framework for any mistakes, which is more straightforward if you have a hearty checking and cautioning framework. In Google Cloud, you can utilize oversaw example gatherings (MIGs) to do A/B or canary testing, just as to play out a moderate rollout or a rollback whenever required.

Configuration questions

How does your improvement group figure out how to construct and delivery?

What coordination and security testing does your advancement group utilize?

How would you move back?

Proposals

Make the CI/CD pipeline the best way to convey to creation.

Confine and secure your CI/CD condition.

Fabricate just a single time and advance the outcome through the pipeline.

Keep your CI/CD pipelines quick.

Limit spreading in your adaptation control framework.

Key administrations

Cloud Source Repositories is a completely included, private Git storehouse administration facilitated on Google Cloud. You can utilize Cloud Source Repositories for community advancement of any application or administration.

Compartment Registry is a solitary spot for your group to oversee Docker pictures, perform weakness investigation, and conclude who can get to what with fine-grained admittance control. Existing CI/CD reconciliations permit you to set up entirely automated Docker pipelines to get quick criticism.

Cloud Build is assistance that executes your expands on the Google Cloud framework. Cloud Build can import source code from GitHub, Bitbucket, Cloud Storage, or Cloud Source Repositories, play out a form to your details, and produce curios, for example, Docker compartments or Java documents.

The DevOps Resource and Assessment (DORA) venture characterizes checking as follows: Monitoring is the way toward gathering, examining, and utilizing the data to follow applications and framework to manage business choices. Observing is an urgent capacity since it gives you understanding into your frameworks and your work. Through observing, you can settle on choices about the effect of changes to your administration, apply the analytical technique to episode reaction, and measure your administration's arrangement with your business objectives. With checking set up, you can do the accompanying:

- Analyze long-term trends.
- Define alerting on critical metrics.
- Compare your experiments over time.

- Perform retrospective analysis.
- Build relevant real-time dashboards.

Screen both business-driven measurements and framework wellbeing measurements. Business-driven measures assist you in seeing how well your frameworks uphold your business. For instance, you could follow the cost to serve a user in an application, the change in volume of traffic to your site following a redesign, or how long it takes a customer to purchase a product on your website. Framework wellbeing measurements assist you with understanding whether your frameworks are working effectively and inside adequate execution levels.

Utilize the accompanying four brilliant signs to screen your framework:

Latency: This is defined as the time the system takes to respond to a request

Traffic: This is defined as the amount of demand placed on your system.

Mistakes: The pace of solicitations that fall flat. Solicitations can bomb expressly (for instance, HTTP 500s), verifiably (for example, an HTTP 200 achievement reaction, however with an inappropriate substance), or by strategy (for example, if you focused on one-second reaction times, any solicitation that takes over one second is a mistake).

Immersion talks about how full your administration is. A proportion of your most obliged assets (That is, in a memory-obliged framework, show memory; in an I/O-compelled framework, show I/O).

Logging

Logging administrations are basic to checking your frameworks. While measurements structure the premise of explicit things to follow, logs contain important data that you requirement for investigating, security-related examination and for consistence necessities. Google Cloud incorporates Cloud Logging, a coordinated logging administration you can use to store, search, analyse, screen, and caution on log information and occasions from Google Cloud. Cloud Logging naturally gathers logs from Google Cloud administrations. You can utilize these logs to manufacture measurements for checking and to make logging fares to outer administrations, for example, Cloud Storage, BigQuery, and Pub/Sub.

Design for disaster recovery

Designing your system to anticipate and handle failure scenarios helps ensure that if there is a catastrophe, the impact on your systems is minimized. To expect failures, make sure you have a well-defined and regularly tested disaster recovery (DR) plan to back up and restore services and data. Service-interrupting events (events that affect the services delivered) can happen at any time. Your network could have an outage, your latest application push might introduce a critical bug, or you might have to contend with a natural disaster. When things go awry, it's essential to have a robust, targeted, and well-tested DR plan.

CONCLUSION/ APPRECIATION

We sincerely appreciate your purchase of our book that reveals useful information about everything you need to know about Google Professional Cloud Architect. We hope you loved it.

Thanks,

Jason Hoffman.

Made in the USA
Monee, IL
11 January 2021

57246022R10174